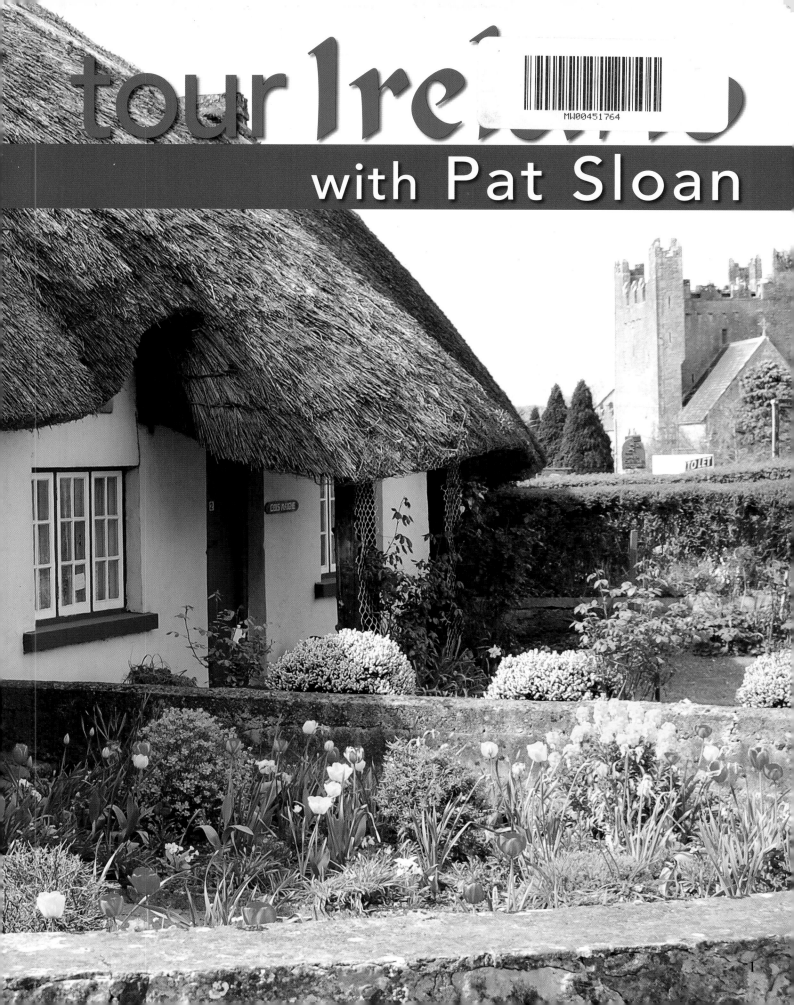

tour Ireland

with Pat Sloan

EDITORIAL TEAM

Sandra Graham Case - Vice President & Editor-in-Chief
Cheryl Nodine Gunnells - Executive Publications Director
Susan White Sullivan - Senior Publications Director
Mark Hawkins - Senior Prepress Director
Debra Nettles - Designer Relations Director
Cheryl Johnson - Quilt Publications Director
Deb Moore - Craft Publications Director
Rhonda Shelby - Art Publications Director
Susan McManus Johnson - Associate Editor
Lisa Lancaster - Technical Editor
Jean Lewis - Technical Writer
Katherine Atchison - Photography Manager
Mark R. Potter - Imaging Technician
Lora Puls - Art Category Manager
Dayle Carozza - Lead Graphic Artist
Amy Gerke - Graphic Artist
Frances Huddleston - Graphic Artist
Jeanne Zaffarano - Graphic Artist
Becky Riddle - Publishing Systems Administrator
Clint Hanson - Publishing Systems Assistant
John Rose - Publishing Systems Assistant
Christy Myers - Photography Stylist
Cheryl Johnson, Jean Lewis, Pam Mayo, Peggy McIntire, Gregg Sloan, and Ken West - Contributing Photographers

BUSINESS STAFF

Tom Siebenmorgen - Vice President & Chief Operations Officer
Pam Stebbins - Vice President of Sales & Marketing
Margaret Reinold - Sales and Service Director
Jim Dittrich - Vice President, Operations
Rob Thieme - Comptroller, Operations
Stan Raynor - Retail Customer Service Manager
Fred F. Pruss - Print Production Manager

PHOTO CREDITS:

Page 30
(Third from top) winner of Royal Society Craft Competition 2006 made by Yuko Kaldenberg
(Fourth from top) voted "Best in Show" First Quarter Exhibition 2006 made by Miriam Gogarty
Page 31
(bottom left) winner of Best Traditional Quilt First Quarter Exhibition 2006 made by Angela Cotter

ISBN-13: 978-1-60140-522-7
ISBN-10: 1-60140-522-7

Table of Contents

6

16

26

COFFEE

52

58

96

Meet Pat Sloan

Photo by Pamela Mayo

Creative and energetic, quilt designer Pat Sloan is well known for her whimsical patterns, innovative books, and fresh, folk-art fabric lines. Her unique style has captured the attention of quilters all over the globe.

In addition to designing, Pat enjoys traveling to and teaching at trade shows, guild meetings, lectures, and quilt shops.

When asked what she does for a living the Herndon, Virginia resident replies, "I design and make quilts for a living, which is a pretty wonderful job."

To see more of Pat's delightful books, patterns, and fabrics, visit her Website at www.quilter'shome.com.

Dear Reader,
I was thrilled when Jim West asked me to host a Quilter's Tour Of Ireland. My husband, Gregg, and I had never been there and wouldn't it be fun to tour Ireland with a group of quilters? What I didn't know, until I got there, was that I *needed* to go to Ireland!

Once we started doing some research we discovered that Sloan is an Irish name and that we have Irish family ties. This fed our interest a bit more.

Once we got to Ireland and met the people, we felt like we had found an entire country of "family." We were warmly welcomed at each and every stop. People were genuinely interested in us and often asked if we were Irish! One lady even told us about an area where the Sloan family might have originated.

It *really* hit me when we visited Cobh. As a major seaport during the great famine of 1845-49, hundreds of thousands of Irish people embarked from Cobh as they fled to America and other countries to start a new life. A life that became part of MY life! It was then I realized that I really am a little bit Irish! The warmth I feel for Ireland and the Irish people is because of the family connections from so many years ago.

I truly feel like I have a new family and home in Ireland. This really was a trip of a lifetime, a trip of wonderful memories, a trip of finding friends I didn't know I had, and a trip of coming "home" to Ireland.

This book is a scrapbook of our Irish journey. Along with my fellow quilters, I learned about Ireland and found new friends in the Irish quilters. The quilts I designed for this book are genuinely Irish inspired. I hope you will follow along, enjoy the tour, make the quilts, and feel a little bit Irish, too.

—Pat

Meet Jim West

Dear Reader,

When I first began talking to Leisure Arts and Pat Sloan about my involvement with this book, I was excited to work on this project for a couple of reasons. First, I think Ireland is a very special place to visit, with its beautiful countryside, charming villages, incredible history, magnificent coastline, lovely people, and of course the fact that they speak English makes it so easy to get around.

The second reason I was so happy to be participating was because this was another opportunity for me to work with Pat. Both Pat and her husband Gregg are special people to be around.

And special is how I would describe our Ireland tour. The ladies who traveled with us on this trip were a real delight. I will even go as far as to say, they were one of the best groups I've ever escorted on a tour. No one was late, no one complained, everyone was cooperative and they all had a great sense of humor. They were a tour director's dream group.

Adding to the success of our tour was our bus driver/guide Mark, who was very knowledgeable and entertaining. Meeting and interacting with the Irish quilters from Killarney and Dublin was a wonderful experience.

Scattered throughout this book, I have provided some helpful travel tips and suggestions to enhance *your* tour, if you ever choose to visit the Emerald Isle. Many of the tips will be useful if you travel anywhere in the world.

It was a real pleasure planning and leading this tour. St. Patrick put it beautifully many centuries ago, *"If I showed forth anything however small, according to God's good pleasure…it was the gift of God."*

May the wind always be at your back and may the good Lord bless your quilting journey.

—Jim

Charismatic and dynamic are two words that come to mind when Jim West's name is mentioned. As founder of Travel Alliance, Inc., parent company of Sew Many Places, his attention to detail and his knack of making each guest feel special have made him one of the most sought-after travel directors in the business.

Among his many credits, Jim is the official travel agent for McCall's Quilting and the American Quilter's Society. He is the author of four cruise/travel books, traveled to 72 countries, and has sailed on over 850 cruises.

To learn more about Jim and his upcoming quilting trips, visit his Website at www.SewManyPlaces.com or call his office toll free at (877) 887-1188.

Photo by Pamela Mayo

Chicago to Killarney

On Monday afternoon our tour officially kicked off at O'Hare International Airport in Chicago.

As passengers arrived in the waiting area, some of us played the "Can You Pick Out The Quilters On Our Trip?" game. Score one point for choosing the lady wearing a quilted jacket! Lose one point for picking the lady with a Bernina tote bag—we never found out where she was headed, but sadly for her, it wasn't with us.

We checked and double-checked to be sure we had our passports, tickets, money, etc. We were ready to go!

Pat's Thoughts:
The first day was a whirlwind of eat and wait, eat and wait.

Colleen, our unofficial mascot.

6

After a brief stop at Dublin Airport, we arrived at **Shannon Airport**, tired, but eager to begin our adventure.

Jim West, owner of Sew Many Places, greeted us. As the tour director for our trip, Jim introduced Mark, our coach driver. Mark graciously babysat our belongings while we exchanged money, had a snack, and just relaxed for a few minutes before boarding the bus for the ride to Killarney.

Once on the bus, Jim asked us to please resist the temptation to take a nap so that we would be able sleep that night and adjust to local time.

Pat's Thoughts:
Ireland was in bloom! The tulips and so many other plants were flowering because of the warm spring.

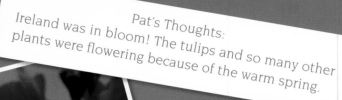

Leaving the airport we drove south, stopping for lunch, sight-seeing, and shopping in the quaint town of **Adare**.

While walking through town, we passed charming shops and businesses housed in picturesque thatched roof cottages.

Being aware of the shortage of fabric shops in Ireland, all of us could hear that cute vacant cottage just crying out to become a quilt shop! Hmmm….

Next stop was **Killarney** and our "home", the beautiful Killarney Plaza Hotel. After receiving instructions to meet at the hotel for dinner, we were free to unpack, shop, or explore the town.

Here are some "touristy" facts about Killarney.
• Killarney is the center of tourism for the southwestern coast of Ireland. It is an excellent home base for day trips in Cork and Kerry Counties.
• Surrounded by sparkling lakes and towering peaks, Killarney sits on the edge of the Killarney National Park.
• Killarney boasts numerous restaurants, pubs, souvenir shops, and historical buildings to explore, but no fabric stores!

At dinner we learned that we were a very geographically diverse bunch. Our group included individuals from Virginia, Ohio, New York, Florida, Washington, Canada, and even Korea! But there was one thing we had in common—we were quilters looking forward to exploring Ireland!

Pat showed us our class project, her *Luck of the Irish Wall Hanging*! Then she shared the exciting news that she had been busy designing quilts for a book about our Ireland trip. She told us that we would be shooting photography on location—with us as models!

After dinner, most of us were ready to call it a day. The next morning would bring the much-anticipated tour of the **Ring of Kerry**, a 170km (106 mile) circular drive around the Kerry Peninsula.

Ring of Kerry

No coaches traveling clockwise here!

On Wednesday we awoke to a beautiful sunny morning, which was very unusual for this time of year! We enjoyed a traditional Irish breakfast at the hotel, including some local favorites such as porridge (a cooked cereal) and black and white pudding (a type of sausage). Was anyone adventurous enough to try the pudding?

As we headed out, Mark explained that all coaches drive around the **Ring of Kerry** in a counterclockwise (or anti-clockwise, if you are Irish) direction. They do this because the road is so narrow in places that it is hard for coaches to pass when going in opposite directions! Maybe that was just a bit of blarney?

Our first stop was by a lovely pasture, overlooking the **Lakes of Killarney** and the towering peaks of the **Mcgillicuddy Reeks**. This beautiful location provided the perfect setting for photographing Pat's *Lady Of The Lake* Quilt. If only the horses hadn't been so camera shy!

Continuing our drive, we passed through the town of **Killorglin,** the gateway to the Ring of Kerry and home to one of Ireland's oldest street festivals, **Puck Fair**. The celebration honors a Puck (or male) goat that, according to legend, alerted the residents to an impending attack by Cromwell in 1649.

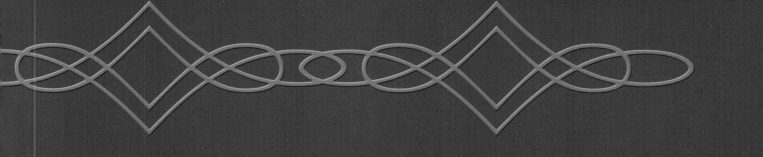

The pretty yellow **gorse flowers** added bright spots of color to the landscape.

Our next stop was near the village of **Glenbeigh** for an Irish Coffee at the **Red Fox Inn**. Here we took advantage of the attractive, ivy-covered pub to snap some photos of Pat with her *Irish Coffee Quilt*.

Irish Coffee, a delicious mixture of coffee, whiskey, sugar, and cream was first introduced in the 1930's. It remains a popular drink throughout Ireland today, as some of our group confirmed!

Located next door to the Red Fox Inn was the **Kerry Bog Village Museum**. A recreation of an 1800's peatland's village, the museum gives visitors a glimpse of daily life during the heyday of peat harvesting. Peatlands, commonly referred to as "bogs" in Ireland, are harvested by digging up strips of decomposed soil. The strips are cut into smaller pieces, allowed to dry, and burned as fuel for heating.

Next on our tour was a stop at **Kells Sheep Centre** where we were introduced to many of the types of sheep that can be found in Ireland. Then we were treated to a fascinating demonstration of sheep herding by Brendan, the Shepherd, and his two border collies. The dogs work together under whistle commands to move the herds to and from the pastures or to separate specific sheep from the herd. The dogs loved all the attention and appeared to be having a great time showing off their skills. And the sheep? Well… it was hard to tell, but they might have preferred to just graze!

Back on the bus we continued towards **Caherdaniel** and our next stop, a delicious lunch at **Scarriff Inn**. The view from the dining room, which overlooks **Scarriff Island** and **Derrynane Bay**, was so beautiful and relaxing that we almost hated to leave, but there was so much more to see!

Pat's Thoughts:
After this stop, I wanted to take home baby lambs and dogs!

12

• As we rounded the southern tip of the peninsula we passed a 10th century farming settlement known as a **ring fort**. The stone or earthenware wall surrounding the community served as an enclosure for domestic animals, protection from wild animals, and a deterrent from human attack.

Pat's Thoughts:
Enjoying a required (yes, REQUIRED) ice cream break in Sneem.

• Our next stop was in the village of **Sneem**, winner of the tidiest village award and home to numerous gift and craft shops that are housed in brightly painted buildings. The knitters in our group were excited to find a shop that sold REAL Irish wool. Still no fabric!

Pat's Thoughts:
The ring drive was breathtaking. We drove past pastures separated by hedges or rock walls, which reminded me of quilt blocks separated by sashings.

Our last stop was **Ladies View**, a popular stopping point overlooking the Lakes of Killarney. The story is told that Queen Victoria's ladies-in-waiting were so enthralled with the view from this spot that it was named after them. No matter how the overlook got its name, the vista was spectacular and *our* ladies were enthralled!

Quilt Workshop
& The Killarney Quilt Guild

After dinner we took part in our first quilt workshop and our get-together with the **Killarney Quilt Guild**. During the workshop Pat explained how she adapts a horizontal design to make it vertical and we learned how to do needleturn appliqué using a running stitch. When Pat finished we all were eager to trace, cut, and stitch on our *Luck Of The Irish* project.

When the members of the Killarney Guild arrived we visited for a while and exchanged small gifts of fabric and patterns. Pat kicked-off Show and Tell with a lecture about designing quilt patterns and fabrics. Then we took turns sharing our quilts and stories. We soon discovered that despite the ocean between us, we had similar quilting styles and tastes.

Quilter's Comments:

"I was struck by how warm and friendly the Irish girls were. There was no hesitation, no awkward silences, just an immediate bonding between the two groups."

"The evening was an overwhelming success as friendships were made and bonds were forged."

"… I felt right at home with both the American and Irish quilters …there were dozens of kindred spirits who didn't think you were strange for fondling fabric …"

"I was surprised by the number of quilters in your (tour) group, I was expecting 4 or 5, not 40!"

Even Mark got into the spirit by playing "Vanna" for us!

Day 4

On Thursday we were greeted by another warm, sunny day for our trip southward through the Cork and Kerry mountains to the seaside city of **Cobh** (pronounced Cove).

Cobh is known as the city with three names. First named Cove, the city was renamed Queenstown in honor of Queen Victoria's visit in 1849. In 1920 it was changed again to Cobh, the Irish spelling of it's original name.

As we toured the **Cobh Heritage Centre** the important role this small seaport played in Irish history unfolded. We learned about the thousands of Irish immigrants who fled from the great famine in search of a better life. We saw exhibits depicting the conditions aboard convict ships bound for Australia. We learned about the ill-fated steam ships, Titanic and Lusitania.

Our walk to the city centre took us past boats of every size and shape anchored in the harbor. There were rows of houses painted in eye-catching shades of pink, purple, peach, and green. Towering above the city we saw the impressive neo-Gothic style **St. Colman's Cathedral**.

After lunch we returned to Killarney where the afternoon was free to shop, sightsee, or stitch on our projects.

Pat's Thoughts:
This was the first time I truly understood how many people left this island—it was millions. And among those millions were our ancestors, which is why a trip to Ireland feels like "coming home" to so many people.

And Back Again

Une exposition poignant

Cobh

Tourist Information
07

Pat's Thoughts:
Guess what surprised me most about Ireland? They have NATIVE palm trees AND they paint their homes bright sherbet colors. I felt like I was in the Caribbean, really!

Queen

We engage
shall be prov
and shall be
on th

Ship to
stown on

17

Friday morning the cool and misty weather was so appropriate for a trip to historic **Blarney Castle**. We were all in high spirits and when Mark put on some lively music, quilters sang along and some even attempted to dance in the aisle of the coach!

Blarney Castle was built by Chieftain Cormac MacCarthy in 1446. After climbing the spiraling, ever narrowing stone staircase we finally reached the top. And there, in the outer wall, was the legendary Blarney Stone! Believed to be half of the Stone of Scone it was used during the coronations of British monarchs. Robert the Bruce presented the stone to MacCarthy for his support during the Battle of Bannockburn, a decisive victory for Scotland during the Wars of Scottish Independence.

Sometimes referred to as The Stone of Eloquence, there are many stories about how the tradition of "Kissing The Blarney Stone" began. One of the more well-known legends states that Queen Elizabeth I wanted all the Irish Chieftains to surrender their land and pledge loyalty to her. Smooth talking MacCarthy always managed to promise compliance without ever taking action. The Queen said that MacCarthy was giving her "a lot of Blarney". The term has come to mean "the ability to speak eloquently without offending" or "insincere talk" and whoever kisses the stone will receive the gift of Blarney.

But…to kiss the stone is not as easy as it sounds. You must lie on your back with someone holding your legs, hang your head upside down, and kiss the stone! Can you believe that *some* members of our group were actually daring enough to perform this feat?

While most of the group was busy exploring the castle and gardens, we were able to get some great photos of Pat's **Irish Chain** quilt. The quilt looked right at home with the impressive castle and beautiful landscape serving as a backdrop.

BLARNEY CASTL
THE HOME OF THE BLARNEY STONE

19

Located just across the town square we discovered **Blarney Woolen Mills**, "The Great Irish Shopping Experience." And, boy, did we shop—Aran sweaters, jewelry, linen, crystal, and china! We managed to do major damage in a short amount of time!

Upon our return to Killarney that afternoon, we were able to choose between going to **Muckross House** or **Ross Castle**.

• **Muckross House** is a Victorian mansion situated within the boundaries of Killarney National Park. Built for the Herbert family in 1843, Muckross House is beautifully furnished in period style. While the upstairs rooms reflect the grandeur of the day, the downstairs houses the servant's quarters and the working heart of the home.

• For those interested in the traditional skills of the era, a visit to the Craft Workshops to see expert craftsmen demonstrating weaving, bookbinding, and pottery-making was a must. Jaunting car rides and tours of the working farm were some of our other choices for our afternoon's excursion.

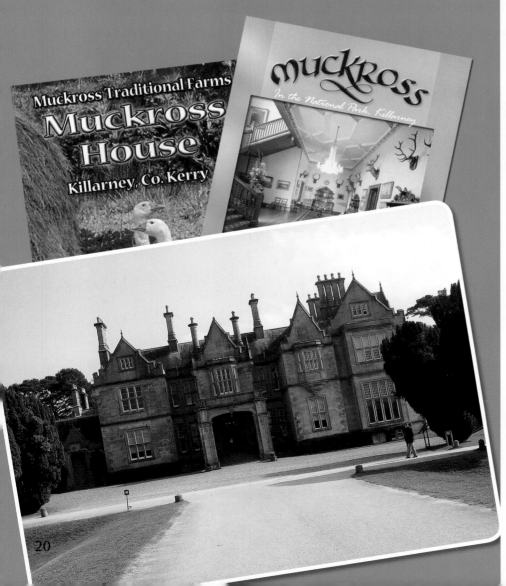

• **Ross Castle**, the ruins of a 15th century tower house, is located on the banks of the Lower Lake of Killarney. The castle was once home to the local chieftains, the O'Donoghues.

• From Ross Castle, we took a relaxing boat ride around the lake to view the spectacular scenery and the ruins of **Muckross Abbey**, founded in 1448 as a Franciscan monastery.

• Following the cruise was a horse-drawn jaunting car ride through **Killarney National Park**. We were convinced that the driver must have kissed the Blarney Stone because of his tale about the leprechaun apartment building! While certainly not true, the stories he told were very entertaining!

Have you seen any leprechauns?

Youghal, Waterford, and Dublin

Saturday morning a light mist was falling as we said goodbye to Killarney and headed towards Dublin.

We took a southwesterly route, stopping in the charming seaside town of **Youghal**, pronounced "yawl" (or "y'all," if you're southern). The town, with its Georgian clock tower and scenic lighthouse, served as the venue for the 1956 version of the movie, *Moby Dick*.

Pat's Thoughts:
The funniest story of this trip, to me, was when someone was trying to put names and faces together. They could not picture which quilter was Colleen... look carefully, she's the one with the pointy nose in this photo!

Our next stop was a factory tour of **Waterford Crystal**, which was founded in 1783. From dainty vases to stunning chandeliers, these world famous makers of fine crystal still produce each piece by *hand*. The Crystal Ball that drops each New Year's Eve in Times Square was made by Waterford in 2000 in honor of the new Millennium.

The informative tour took us through each stage of the manufacturing process from melting the components to the final polishing. Everyone was impressed by the attention to detail and the beauty of the finished pieces. The tour of the gallery gave us the opportunity to view some of their magnificent pieces. After lunch and a quick shopping spree in the gift shop we continued on to Dublin.

Pat's Thoughts:
The tour of Waterford was amazing...
a "must do" on a trip to Ireland!

As we entered **Dublin** we saw a modern city, which has managed to retain most of its old world charm. Checking in to our new home, The Burlington, we were struck by the differences in the atmosphere of this lively, cosmopolitan hotel and the more relaxed feel of the Killarney Plaza.

After dinner Pat and Gregg took a walk to the city centre. They found the city very much alive with people strolling through the parks, shopping on Grafton Street, and partying in the Temple Bar area.

Here are some "touristy" facts about the city of Dublin.
• Founded in the 9th century by the Vikings, Dublin is the capital and largest city in Ireland.
• The River Liffey, which flows from east to west, splits the city in half. The Liffey and Poodle rivers converge to form a dark colored harbor, giving rise to the name Dublin or "black pool."
• Dublin boasts many historical sites, city parks, shopping areas, and an abundance of pubs, restaurants, and entertainment venues.

Pat's Thoughts:
Dublin at night is THE place to be! It was so vibrant and the people watching was the best!

Dublin Visitor Map used by kind permission of Pat Liddy

Avoca & Glendalough

Sunday morning we were greeted with slightly cooler temperatures and a light misty rain as we headed southeast towards the **Wicklow Mountains**. Know as the **Garden of Ireland**, County Wicklow is well known for its popularity as a movie location.

Nestled between towering mountain peaks and lush woodlands lies the picturesque village of **Avoca**. Our excursion to **Avoca Handweavers**, the oldest working woolen mill in Ireland, turned out to be one of the most enjoyable stops of our trip.

We took an informative tour of the weaving shed, where we saw the handlooms in action, had fun selecting scraps of yarn to bring home, and met another group of Americans who were on a knitting tour of Ireland!

We explored the cluster of charming whitewashed buildings that house the mill (complete with a shop dog), gift shop (where we left lots of our money), and café (mmm…pie)! The misty rain had stopped so we were able to photograph several of Pat's quilts, including, **Sheep On The Mountain** and the **With Needle and Thread** sewing case.

• We continued on through the **Vale of Avoca**, to the site made famous by Thomas Moore's poem **The Meeting Of The Waters**. After just a brief stop in this serene spot, where the Avoca and Avonbeg Rivers come together, we could certainly appreciate Moore's sentiment when he wrote the following verse:

> "Sweet Vale of Avoca how
> calm I could rest
> In thy bosom of shade with the
> friends I love best
> When the storms that we feel
> in this cold world should cease
> And our hearts like thy waters
> be mingled in peace"

Our next stop was the village of **Glendalough** (which means the valley of the two lakes) and St. Kevin's Monastery. Originally founded in the 6th century the monastic site has been plagued by centuries of ill fortune including fire, plunder, and war. Among the ruins are a stone church, a cemetery with beautiful Celtic cross headstones, and a stone **round tower**.

Built around the time of the Viking invasions (about 1066AD), the original purpose of the round tower has been the subject of debate. Some historians believe the tower was designed to be a place of refuge from attack while others think it was simply a belfry.

After a quick jaunt up the hill (it turned out be farther than we thought!) to see one of the lakes and snap a few photos, we hurried back to the waiting bus.

Heading north toward Dublin, we drove past lush green fields where sheep and lambs grazed contentedly. We ooohed and aaahed over the lambs. In fact, we whined, begged, and someone even sent Mark a note asking him to please stop for photos and…he did!

Pat's Thoughts:
Yes, there are sheep in Ireland.
Lots and lots of sheep!

When we returned to Dublin Mark recommended O'Neill's Pub or Leo Burdock's Fish and Chips for a traditional Irish lunch. Thumbs up on the food from both places!

After lunch, we headed to the famed Grafton Street area for an afternoon of shopping and sightseeing. There we found the first and only real fabric shop of our trip! The store carried a large variety of textiles, including a small amount of fabric for quilting. But…it was fabric!

Actually, we had been having so much fun with all our activities that we really hadn't time to think TOO much about fabric shops!

In spite of the scattered showers, we had a fun afternoon exploring the shops, street vendors, and parks. We even managed to get a few shots of Pat's **Streets of Ireland** quilt.

Quilt Workshop & The Dublin Quilt Guild

Pat's workshop that night was based on her book, **Learn to Bead With Pat Sloan**. We had a lot of fun practicing our beading techniques. Pat suggested we try out our new skills by beading on our **Luck Of The Irish** wall hangings. How cute!

After class, Deirde, the Chairperson of the Eastern Branch of the Irish Patchwork Society, Mary, the representative to the European Quilt Association, and thirteen of the Society's members, joined us. There are seven branches of the Irish Patchwork Society scattered throughout Ireland with the Eastern Branch being the largest.

Pat began the evening's program with a short lecture about designing and quilting. Then she gave us a sneak preview of some of the quilts she designed for this book.

During Show and Tell we were amazed by the beautiful quilts the Irish ladies had made. An extra treat for us was the opportunity to see some of their competition quilts from the 25th Anniversary National Exhibition. WOW! What lovely and creative work!

Following Show and Tell we shared our fat quarters and other small gifts. Two thoughtful Irish quilters, sisters Angela and Enda, gave each of us a loaf of homemade brown bread, complete with pats of butter and jars of jam! We visited and talked "quilt" until very late, as we had so much to share.

Brown Bread
Ingredients: Course Wholemeal, Porridge, Wheatgerm, Bran, Olive oil, Honey, Buttermilk
Bread Soda
Enjoy - From: Irish Patchwork Society

Quilter's Comments:
"One comment (from an American quilter) that I liked was, 'such wonderful work and no fabric shops!' We do have a growing number of shops so the work should be even better next time you come."

"I struck up a conversation with a lady from Japan who now lives in Dublin…her quilting was beautiful. …how awesome that I had an opportunity to share my life and love (of quilting) with someone across the world and find common threads within our separate lives."

"I chatted with an Irish quilter who comes to America several times a year to see her daughter in Indiana. She loves to visit our quilt shops and always stocks up on supplies when she is in the States."

Pat's Thoughts:
I would love to go back and spend a whole day doing a retreat with our group and the Irish quilters. That would really allow us the time to get to know each other.

Dublin City Tour

On Monday a light, cool rain fell as we left for our bus tour of Dublin. Our city guide pointed out sights of interest such as the eye-catching facades of the Georgian District, the historic Christ Church Cathedral, and the American Embassy.

THE NATIONAL CATHEDRAL AND COLLEGIATE CHURCH OF ST PATRICK ❖ DUBLIN

SIGILL... CAPITVLI CANO...

The Dean and Chapter welcome you and thank you for your gift

EMBASSY OF THE UNITED STATES OF AMERICA

Our first stop was **St. Patrick's Cathedral.** Established in 1191 it is the oldest cathedral in Ireland. The present day church was rebuilt in the 13th century and underwent a total restoration between 1860 and 1900.

St. Patrick's is an active center of worship with services held there every day. We were fortunate to arrive as the choir was rehearsing and what a moving experience!

Located on the grounds and in the sanctuary are numerous monuments to past church and civic leaders and the military. The banners above the choir stall commemorate the Knights of St. Patrick.

The beautiful tile floors were definitely inspiring to our group of quilters. We could easily visualize appliqué or quilting patterns based on the designs found in the floors.

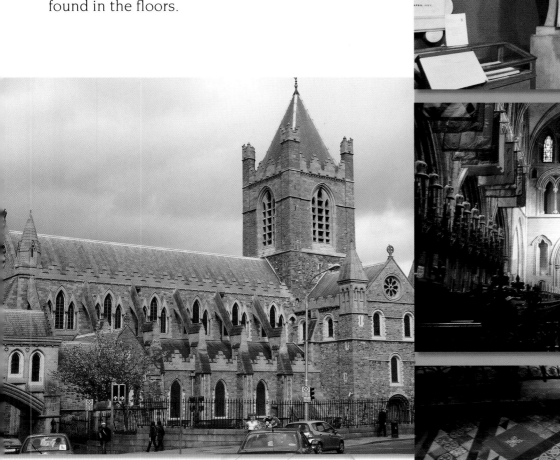

Our next stop was **Trinity College**. Founded in 1592, it is the oldest university in Ireland. The Trinity College Library is home to the **Book of Kells**, a lavishly decorated Latin manuscript of the four gospels. The Celtic-style illustrations were just beautiful, but unfortunately photography was not allowed. To learn more about The Book of Kells go to www.tcd.ie/info/trinity/bookofkells/.

Next on the tour was a brief stop at **Dublin Castle** where we saw part of the original city wall that surrounded Dublin in Viking times. This section known as The Arch was constructed in 1240AD. Through the years the castle has served a multitude of functions including a royal residence, military installation, and a prison. Today the castle has been completely restored and houses a conference centre, library, arts centre, and is a venue for state functions.

Continuing on we drove through **Phoenix Park**, home of the **Dublin Zoo,** and largest park in Europe. Located within the park are the residences of the President of Ireland and the American Ambassador to Ireland.

The last stop of the day was a self-guided walking tour of the **Guinness Brewery**. The tour concluded with a free sample of Guinness and for those who really liked the sample more could be purchased in the roof top bar. The bar offered a breathtaking 360° panoramic view of Dublin and even if you didn't need more Guinness, it was well worth the trek to the top.

That night, Jim hosted a limerick contest, complete with prizes. What fun! Limericks are five-line poems in which lines 1, 2, and 5 rhyme and lines 3 and 4 rhyme. Although there is no real documentation of its origin, the Irish are masters of this type of poetry. Some of our entries were amusing, some poked fun, and some echoed our feelings about Ireland.

Here's one of the winning entries:
Sweet Ireland, so lush and so green.
Glitterin' seascapes like you've ne'er seen.
Dancin' round the Ring of Kerry,
Perchance to glimpse leprechaun or fairy.
Ah, Ireland, prettiest place I've e'er been.

Following the contest we gathered in the hotel restaurant for our last dinner as a group. After dinner some of us made a final trip downtown while some tried to figure how to pack all of our purchases! It didn't seem like THAT much when we were shopping—maybe our belongings just multiplied, like hangers in a closet!

Dublin to Chicago

What do you mean you went shopping again? I told you there was no space left!

On Tuesday morning, we headed to Dublin Airport where we unfortunately had to say goodbye to Mark. Before catching our flight to Chicago, we had the chance to visit, eat lunch, or do a little last minute shopping (as if we needed any more stuff!).

When we landed in Chicago there was a flurry of activity as we promised to keep in touch, said our goodbyes, and rushed off in different directions to catch our connecting flights home.

The trip to Ireland was an incredible experience and a large part of that was due to the dynamics of our group. Pat and Gregg went out of their way to make each of us feel welcome and special. Jim made sure things ran smoothly and that every need was met quickly and professionally. Mark was funny, helpful, and a joy to be around. Our fellow travelers were so open and friendly that it didn't take long to get to know and feel comfortable with each other. In the end, we all agreed that we could hardly wait for the next trip…hmmm…maybe England, Italy, or France?

Remember Colleen, What happens in Ireland stays in Ireland.

Pat's Thoughts:
The people of Ireland are warm, friendly, and want to be sure you feel welcomed. Besides the country being beautiful, the people are, too…what can be better than that?

Pat's Thoughts:
It was hard to leave…I really needed a month there, no kidding. Just as I was getting into it, we had to go!

Aer Lingus

HEAVY
WEIGHT Kgs
23

Now that you've seen some of Ireland's prettiest places, friendliest faces, and some sheep along the way, you're ready to start your very own Irish quilt adventure...

Jim's Travel Tip:
When traveling to Ireland be sure to bring a converter to change the electrical current from 220 volts to 110 and an adaptor designed for use in Irish wall sockets.

Blooms of

I fell in love with an Irish wildflower called the Mountain Avens, which grows in a rocky and windswept area of Ireland. Despite its bleak surroundings the little flower is just so cheerful! These low growing plants can bloom anytime from April to October with the peak season usually occurring in May.

Ireland

Even though the real blossoms are actually creamy white with golden centers, I chose to make my quilt from these beautiful peach fabrics. I was inspired by some antique quilts to use a four-block setting, which makes this quilt the perfect size for a wall hanging.

To have a bit of Ireland at home, I think I'm going to plant a few Mountain Avens in my yard!

May the road rise to met you,
May the wind always be at your back,
May the sun shine warmly on your face,
The rains fall softly on your fields and,
Until we meet again,
May God hold you in the palm
of His hand.

Finished Quilt Size: 51" x 51" (130 cm x 130 cm)
Finished Block Size: 18" x 18" (46 cm x 46 cm)

FABRIC REQUIREMENTS

Yardage is based on 43"/44" (109 cm/112 cm) wide fabric.

1¼ yds (1.1 m) of cream stripe fabric for backgrounds

⅝ yd (57 cm) of peach floral print fabric for sashing and appliqués

1 yd (91 cm) of peach dot print fabric for borders and appliqués

⅞ yd (80 cm) of brown print fabric for sashing square, borders, and binding

1 yd (91 cm) of green print fabric for appliqués

¼ yd (23 cm) of peach print fabric for appliqués

11" x 11" (28 cm x 28 cm) piece of multi-color stripe fabric for appliqués

8" x 8" (20 cm x 20 cm) piece of yellow print fabric for appliqués

6" x 6" (15 cm x 15 cm) piece of rust print fabric for appliqués

3⅜ yds (3.1 m) of fabric for backing

You will also need:

59" x 59" (150 cm x 150 cm) piece of batting

Paper-backed fusible web

Stabilizer or spray starch

CUTTING THE PIECES

*Follow **Rotary Cutting**, page 120, to cut fabric. Cut all strips from the selvage-to-selvage width of the fabric. All measurements include ¹/₄" seam allowances.*

From cream stripe fabric:
- Cut 2 strips 20" wide. From these strips, cut 4 **backgrounds** 20" x 20".

From peach floral print fabric:
- Cut 2 strips 4¹/₂" wide. From these strips, cut 4 **sashings** 4¹/₂" x 18¹/₂".

From peach dot fabric:
- Cut 3 strips 5⁷/₈" wide. From these strips, cut 16 **squares** 5⁷/₈" x 5⁷/₈".
- Cut 1 strip 5¹/₂" wide. From this strip, cut 4 **corner squares** 5¹/₂" x 5¹/₂".

From brown print fabric:
- Cut 3 strips 5⁷/₈" wide. From these strips, cut 16 **squares** 5⁷/₈" x 5⁷/₈".
- Cut 1 **sashing square** 4¹/₂" x 4¹/₂".
- Cut 6 **binding strips** 1¹/₂" wide.

CUTTING THE APPLIQUÉS

*Patterns, page 43, are reversed and do not include seam allowances. Follow **Preparing Fusible Appliqués**, page 122, to cut appliqués.*

From peach floral print fabric:
- Cut 12 petals (**D**).
- Cut 5 buds (**A**).

From peach dot print fabric:
- Cut 11 petals (**D**).
- Cut 6 buds (**A**).

From green print fabric:
- Cut 16 leaves (**C**).
- Cut 16 bud caps (**B**).

From peach print fabric:
- Cut 9 petals (**D**).
- Cut 5 buds (**A**).

From multi-color stripe fabric:
- Cut 4 large circles (**E**).

From yellow print fabric:
- Cut 4 medium circles (**F**).

From rust print fabric:
- Cut 4 small circles (**G**).

ADDING THE APPLIQUÉS

*Refer to **Machine Blanket Stitch Appliqué**, page 122, for technique.*

1. Arrange appliqués on background working from background to forefront in alphabetical order; fuse in place.
2. Machine Blanket Stitch Appliqué pieces to background to make **Block**. Make 4 Blocks.

Block (make 4)

3. Centering appliqués, trim each Block to 18¹/₂" x 18¹/₂".

ASSEMBLING THE QUILT TOP CENTER

*Follow **Piecing** and **Pressing**, page 121, to assemble quilt top. Use ¹/₄" seam allowances throughout.*

1. Sew 2 **Blocks** and 1 **sashing** together to make **Row A**. Make 2 Row A's.
2. Sew 2 **sashings** and 1 **sashing square** together to make **Row B**.
3. Sew **Row A's** and **Row B** together to complete quilt top center.

ADDING THE BORDERS

1. Draw a diagonal line on wrong side of each peach dot **square**. With right sides together, place 1 peach dot square on top of 1 brown print **square**. Stitch ¹/₄" from each side of line (**Fig. 1**).

Fig. 1

2. Cut along drawn line. Open up and press to make 2 **Triangle-Squares**. Make 32 Triangle-Squares.

Triangle-Squares (make 32)

3. Sew 8 **Triangle-Squares** together to make **Border**. Make 4 Borders.

Border (make 4)

4. Sew 1 **Border** to the top and bottom of the quilt top center.
5. Sew a peach dot **corner square** to the end of each remaining Border.
6. Sew 1 Border to each side of the quilt top center.

FINISHING THE QUILT

1. Following **Quilting**, page 124, to mark, layer, and quilt. Pat's quilt is quilted with feathers in the block backgrounds. The borders are quilted with big loopy flowers and there are veins quilted in the petals.
2. Refer to **Making a Hanging Sleeve**, page 126, to make and attach a hanging sleeve, if desired.
3. Use **binding strips** and follow **Making Straight-Grain Binding**, page 126, to make binding. Follow **Pat's Machine-Sewn Binding**, page 126, to bind quilt.

Jim's Travel Tip:
Even though most hotels offer a "wake up" call, it is advisable to bring a battery operated alarm clock or a cell phone with an alarm.

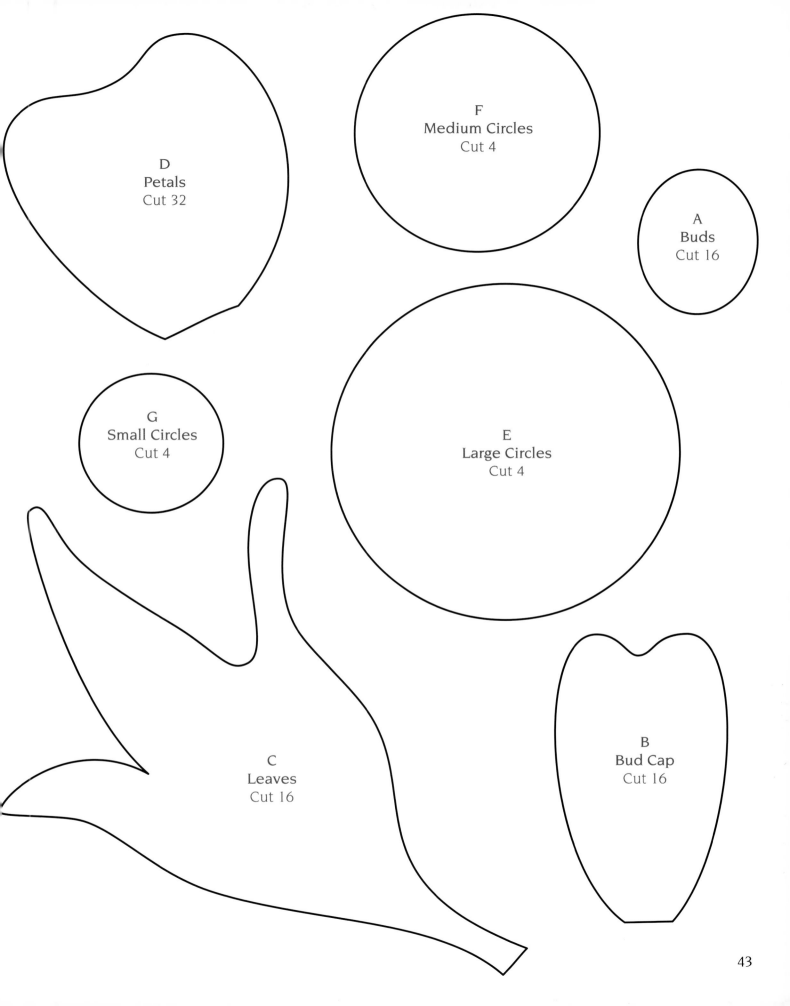

D
Petals
Cut 32

F
Medium Circles
Cut 4

A
Buds
Cut 16

G
Small Circles
Cut 4

E
Large Circles
Cut 4

C
Leaves
Cut 16

B
Bud Cap
Cut 16

Cobblestones of Ireland

There are some very interesting road construction techniques to be found in older cities, like cobblestone streets. While you do see a few cobblestone streets in some American cities, they are everywhere in Ireland!

This quilt, with its checkerboard squares and decorative sashings, was inspired by the patterns I saw in the cobblestones—a simple yet effective design.

I chose a purple pansy print as my main fabric to remind me of the flowers I saw blooming everywhere. As if I really could forget that awesome sight!

Jim's Travel Tip:
On most bus tours in Ireland your driver is also your tour guide. It is a nice gesture to bring a special gift for him, especially something common to your area, i.e. maple syrup from Vermont, Hershey chocolates from Pennsylvania.

Finished Size: 69" x 69" (175 cm x 175 cm)
Finished Block Size: 15" x 15" (38 cm x 38 cm)

FABRIC REQUIREMENTS

Yardage is based on 43"/44" (109 cm/112 cm) wide fabric.

2 yds (1.8 m) of peach print fabric

⁵/₈ yd (57 cm) of purple dot print fabric

1¼ yds (1.1 m) of purple medium floral print fabric

⁵/₈ yd (57 cm) of green print fabric for middle border and binding

2¹/₈ yds (1.9 m) of purple large floral print fabric

4³/₈ yds (4 m) of fabric for backing

You will also need:

77" x 77" (196 cm x 196 cm) square of batting

CUTTING THE PIECES

Follow Rotary Cutting, page 120, to cut fabric. Cut all strips from the selvage-to-selvage width of the fabric unless otherwise noted. All measurements include 1/4" seam allowances. Cutting lengths for borders include an extra 4" of length for "insurance." Borders will be trimmed to fit after measuring completed quilt top center.

From peach print fabric:
- Cut 4 **strips** 3½" wide.
- Cut 3 strips 5⅞" wide. From these strips, cut 18 **large squares** 5⅞" x 5⅞".
- Cut 1 strip 5½" wide. From this strip, cut 4 **medium squares** 5½" x 5½" for the inner border corners.
- Cut 8 strips 3½" wide. From these strips, cut 88 **small squares** 3½" x 3½".

From purple dot print fabric:
- Cut 5 strips 3½" wide.

From purple medium floral print fabric:
- Cut 9 strips 3½" wide. From these strips, cut 36 **rectangles** 3½" x 9½".
- Cut 2 strips 3½" wide. From these strips, cut 20 **small squares** 3½" x 3½".

From green print fabric:
- Cut 6 **middle border strips** 1" wide.
- Cut 8 **binding strips** 1½" wide.

From purple large floral print fabric:
- Cut 2 *lengthwise* **top/bottom outer borders** 6½" x 60½".
- Cut 2 *lengthwise* **side outer borders** 6½" x 72½".

From remaining width:
- Cut 9 strips 5⅞"wide. From these strips, cut 18 **large squares** 5⅞" x 5⅞".

Jim's Travel Tip:
Ireland is green for one reason and one reason only—it rains a lot! Be sure you pack an umbrella.

ASSEMBLING THE BLOCKS

Follow **Piecing** *and* **Pressing**, *page 121, to assemble the blocks. Use ¹/₄" seam allowances throughout.*

Cobblestone Block

1. Sew 2 purple dot print **strips** and 1 peach print **strip** together to make **Strip Set A**. Make 2 Strip Set A's. Cut across Strip Set A's at 3¹/₂" intervals to make 18 **Unit 1's**.

Strip Set A (make 2)   **Unit 1** (make 18)

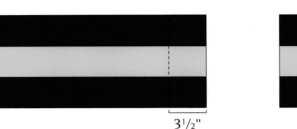

3¹/₂"

2. Sew 2 peach print **strips** and 1 purple dot print **strip** together to make **Strip Set B**. Cut across Strip Set B at 3¹/₂" intervals to make 9 **Unit 2's**.

Strip Set B   **Unit 2** (make 9)

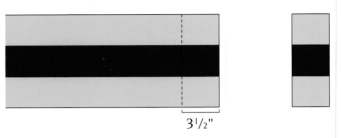

3¹/₂"

3. Sew 2 Unit 1's and 1 Unit 2 together to make **Nine-Patch Unit**. Make 9 Nine-Patch Units.

Nine-Patch Unit (make 9)

Good shopping, girls!

48

4. Place 1 peach print **small square** on 1 end of 1 **rectangle** and stitch diagonally (**Fig. 1**). Trim ¼" from stitching line (**Fig. 2**). Open up and press, pressing seam allowances toward darker fabric (**Fig. 3**).

Fig. 1

Fig. 2

Fig. 3

5. Place 1 peach print **small square** on opposite end of **rectangle**. Stitch and trim as shown in **Fig. 4**. Open and press to make **Unit 3**. Make 36 Unit 3's.

Fig. 4

Unit 3 (make 36)

6. Referring to **Block Diagrams**, sew Nine-Patch Units, Unit 3's, and **small squares** together to make **Blocks**.

Block A (make 4)

Block B (make 4)

Block C (make 1)

ASSEMBLING THE QUILT TOP CENTER

1. Rotating Blocks as needed, sew 2 **Block A's** and 1 **Block B** together to make **Row A**. Make 2 Row A's.
2. Rotating Blocks as needed, sew 2 **Block B's** and 1 **Block C** together to make **Row B**.
3. Rotating Rows as needed, sew Rows A and B together to make quilt top center.

ADDING THE BORDERS

1. Draw a diagonal line on wrong side of each peach print **large square**. With right sides together, place 1 peach large square on top of 1 purple large floral print **large square**. Stitch seam $^1/_4$" from each side of drawn line (**Fig. 4**).

Fig. 4

2. Cut along drawn line and press seam allowances to darker fabric to make 2 **Triangle-Squares**. Make 36 Triangle-Squares.

Triangle-Square (make 36)

3. Sew 9 Triangle-Squares together to make **Inner Border**. Make 4 Inner Borders.

Inner Border (make 4)

4. Sew an inner border to the top and bottom of the quilt top center.
5. Sew 1 peach **medium square** to each end of each remaining inner border.
6. Sew remaining inner borders to the sides of the quilt top center.
7. Using diagonal seams (**Fig. 5**), sew **middle border strips** together end to end to make 1 continuous middle border strip.

Fig. 5

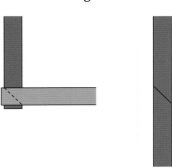

8. To determine length of top/bottom middle borders, measure **width** of quilt top center. From middle border strip, cut 2 **top/bottom middle borders** the determined length. Matching centers and corners, sew top/bottom middle borders to quilt top. Press seam allowances toward borders.
9. To determine length of side middle borders, measure **length** (including added borders) of quilt top center. From middle border strip, cut 2 **side middle borders** the determined length. Matching centers and corners, sew side middle borders to quilt top center. Press seam allowances toward borders.
10. Repeat **Steps 8-9** to add outer borders.

FINISHING THE QUILT

1. Following **Quilting**, page 124, to mark, layer, and quilt. Pat's quilt is machine quilted with an X across each Nine-Patch Unit and leaves in the peach squares of each Nine-Patch Unit. There are ribbon swirls in each "star point" around the outside of the quilt top center and curved outline quilting in the remaining "star points." There are flowers in the purple medium print area where the corners of 4 blocks join and feathers in the remaining purple medium print areas. Flower petals and leaves are quilted in the inner borders with a complete flower quilted in the corner square. The outer border is meander quilted with leaves and tendrils.

2. Refer to **Making A Hanging Sleeve**, page 126, to make and attach a hanging sleeve, if desired.

3. Use **binding strips** and follow **Making Straight-Grain Binding**, page 126, to make binding. Follow **Pat's Machine-Sewn Binding**, page 126, to bind quilt.

Jim's Travel Tip:
When you are packing breakable purchases to bring home, wrap them in a sweater or jacket and place them in the center of your luggage. You might even consider bringing some bubble wrap from home.

Irish Coffee

As I was researching Ireland, I began to wonder if the delicious and soothing drink called Irish Coffee was really invented in Ireland. Here's the story I found.

In the 1930s and 1940s, Foynes, a port town in the southwest of Ireland, was a major transfer point for travelers between the United States and Europe. Arriving at the terminal after an eighteen-hour seaplane flight and short boat trip, passengers were often cold and exhausted.

Brendan O'Regan, manager of the Foynes terminal restaurant, realized that the passengers might appreciate being welcomed with a strong, hot beverage. His chef, Joe Sheridan, took on the challenge to develop a drink that would warm traveler's hearts and spirits.

The story goes, that after tasting the new drink, one of the passengers asked, "Is this Brazilian coffee?" to which Joe replied, "No, that's Irish coffee." And so the name, Irish Coffee, was born! Hmmm?

If you travel through Shannon Airport today, keep your eyes open for the plaque commemorating Joe's creation. And don't forget to stop into The Sheridan Bar in the Departures Lounge for an Irish Coffee, which is still being made from his original recipe.

May you live as long as you want, and never want as long as you live.

I'm certain that you just can't wait to try out this legendary recipe – enjoy!

IRISH COFFEE
1 shot Irish whiskey
1 teaspoon raw sugar
1 heaping spoonful whipped cream
Strong, hot coffee

Pre-warm a stemmed glass. Pour in the whiskey. Add sugar and coffee. Float the whipped cream on top. Don't stir! Enjoy the true flavor by sipping your drink through the whipped cream.

Jim's Travel Tip:
Many hotels in Ireland provide only a minimal number of hangers. Since plastic hangers weigh very little it is advisable to pack some, especially if you will be sharing a room.

Jim's Travel Tip:
Your hotel may offer all kinds of brochures from companies wanting you to participate in their tours or visit their business. Some of these excursions can really enhance your trip. Be sure to look at these on the first day of your tour.

Finished Quilt Size: 21¹/₂" x 26¹/₂" (55 cm x 67 cm)

FABRIC REQUIREMENTS

Yardage is based on 43"/44" (109 cm/112 cm) wide fabric.

11¹/₂" x 15¹/₂" (29 cm x 39 cm) rectangle of cream stripe fabric
4¹/₂" x 15¹/₂" (11 cm x 39 cm) rectangle of tan print fabric
5¹/₂" x 15¹/₂" (14 cm x 39 cm) rectangle of dark red print fabric
³/₈ yd (34 cm) of green print fabric #1 (includes binding)
10" x 15" (25 cm x 38 cm) rectangle of green print fabric #2
¹/₄ yd (23 cm) of brown print fabric #1
7" x 12" (18 cm x 30 cm) rectangle of brown print fabric #2
4" x 6" (10 cm x 15 cm) piece of cream print fabric
³/₄ yd (69 cm) of fabric for backing

You will also need:

26" x 31" (66 cm x 79 cm) rectangle of batting
Paper-backed fusible web
Stabilizer or spray starch

CUTTING THE PIECES

Follow **Rotary Cutting**, *page 120, to cut fabric. Cut all strips from the selvage-to-selvage width of the fabric. All measurements include* 1/4" *seam allowances.*

From green print fabric #1:
- Cut 2 **side inner borders** 1" x 20½".
- Cut 2 **top/bottom inner borders** 1" x 16½".
- Cut 4 **binding strips** 1½"w.

From brown print fabric #1:
- Cut 4 **outer borders** 3" x 21½".

CUTTING THE APPLIQUÉS

Patterns, pages 56 and 57, are reversed and do not include seam allowances. Follow **Preparing Fusible Appliqués**, *page 122, to cut appliqués.*

From green print fabric #1:
- Cut 1 **mug handle** (**A**).
- Cut 1 **mug base** (**B**).

From green print fabric #2:
- Cut 3 **pub sign strips** 1" x 8" (**E**).
- Cut **letters** to spell **COFFEE**.

From brown print fabric #2:
- Cut **letters** to spell **IRISH**.
- Cut 1 **mug** (**D**).

From cream print fabric:
- Cut 1 **whipped cream** (**C**).

ASSEMBLING THE QUILT TOP

Follow **Piecing** *and* **Pressing**, *page 121, to assemble quilt top. Use* 1/4" *seam allowances throughout.*

1. Sew cream stripe and tan print **rectangles** together to make **Unit 1**.

Unit 1

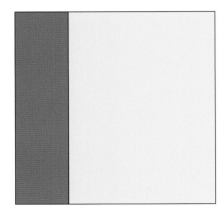

2. Sew dark red print **rectangle** to the bottom edge of Unit 1 to make quilt top center.

Quilt Top Center

ADDING THE APPLIQUÉS

Refer to **Machine Blanket Stitch Appliqué**, *page 122, for technique.*

1. Arrange appliqué pieces on quilt top center working from background to forefront in alphabetical order; fuse in place.
2. Machine Blanket Stitch Appliqué pieces to quilt top center.

FINISHING THE QUILT

1. Sew **side** then **top/bottom inner borders** to quilt top center.
2. Sew **side** then **top/bottom outer borders** to quilt top center.
3. Follow **Quilting**, page 124, to mark, layer, and quilt as desired. Pat's quilt is quilted with a widely spaced loop pattern in the background and outer border. There is outline quilting around the appliqués. The whipped cream has echo quilting repeating the shape and the pub strips have waves down the centers.
4. Refer to **Making a Hanging Sleeve**, page 126, to make and attach a hanging sleeve, if desired.
5. Use **binding strips** and follow **Making Straight-Grain Binding**, page 126, to make binding. Follow **Pat's Machine-Sewn Binding**, page 126, to bind quilt.

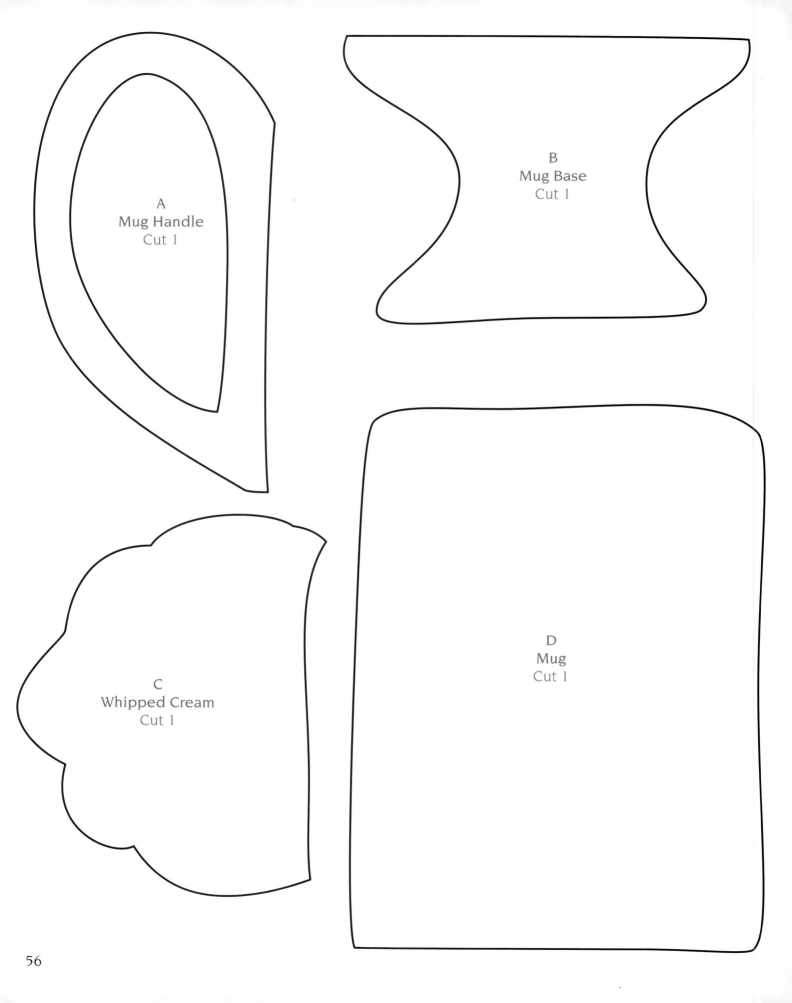

A
Mug Handle
Cut 1

B
Mug Base
Cut 1

C
Whipped Cream
Cut 1

D
Mug
Cut 1

Lady of the Lake

Our tour took us past lake after lake. We even took a boat ride on Lough Leane (Lower Lake) past Ross Castle and the ruins of Muckross Abbey. The deep blue of the water and the clear blue of the sky were amazing. I wanted to capture that image in fabric so I chose prints in shades of blue and used the traditional Lady of the Lake block for this quilt.

Finished Quilt Size: 52" x 52" (132 cm x 132 cm)
Finished Block Size: 12" x 12" (30 cm x 30 cm)

FABRIC REQUIREMENTS

Yardage is based on 43"/44" (109 cm/112 cm) wide fabric.

1¹/₈ yds (1 m) of navy print #1 fabric for water and binding

⁷/₈ yd (80 cm) of navy print #2 fabric for water and Triangle-Squares

⁵/₈ yd (57 cm) of light blue floral print fabric for sky

³/₈ yd (34 cm) **each** of medium blue print #1 fabric and medium blue print #2 fabric for Triangle-Squares

1¹/₂ yds (1.4 m) of yellow floral print fabric for setting triangles

3³/₈ yds (3.1 m) of fabric for backing

You will also need;

60" x 60" (152 cm x 152 cm) piece of batting

CUTTING THE PIECES

*Follow **Rotary Cutting**, page 120, to cut fabric. Cut all strips from the selvage-to-selvage width of the fabric. All measurements include ¹/₄" seam allowances.*

From navy print #1:

- Cut 2 strips 12⁷/₈" wide. From these strips, cut 4 squares 12⁷/₈" x 12⁷/₈". Cut each square **once** diagonally to make 8 **large triangles.**
- Cut 6 **binding strips** 1¹/₂" wide.

From navy print #2:

- Cut 1 strip 12⁷/₈" wide. From this strip, cut 3 squares 12⁷/₈" x 12⁷/₈". Cut each square **once** diagonally to make 6 **large triangles.** You will use 5 large triangles and discard 1.
- Cut 5 strips 2⁷/₈" wide. From these strips, cut 59 **squares** 2⁷/₈" x 2⁷/₈" for Triangle-Squares.

From light blue floral print:
- Cut 2 strips 8⅞" wide. From these strips, cut 7 squares 8⅞" x 8⅞". Cut each square in half once diagonally to make 14 **medium triangles**. You will use 13 medium triangles and discard 1.

From medium blue print #1:
- Cut 3 strips 2⅞" wide. From these strips, cut 29 **squares** 2⅞" x 2⅞" for Triangle-squares.
- Cut 1 strip 2⅞" wide. From this strip, cut 8 squares 2⅞" x 2⅞". Cut each square in half once diagonally to make 16 **small triangles**.

From medium blue print #2:
- Cut 3 strips 2⅞" wide. From these strips, cut 30 **squares** 2⅞" x 2⅞" for Triangle-squares.
- Cut 1 strip 2⅞" wide. From this strip, cut 5 squares 2⅞" x 2⅞". Cut each square in half once diagonally to make 10 **small triangles**.

From yellow floral print:
- Cut 2 strips 18¼" wide. From these strips, cut 4 squares 18¼" x 18¼". Cut each square in half twice diagonally to make 8 **side setting triangles**.
- Cut 1 strip 9⅜" wide. From this strip, cut 2 squares 9⅜" x 9⅜". Cut each square **once** diagonally to make 4 **corner setting triangles**.

ASSEMBLING THE BLOCKS

Follow **Piecing** *and* **Pressing**, *page 121, to assemble the blocks. Use ¼" seam allowances throughout.*

1. Draw a diagonal line on wrong side of each medium blue print **square**. With right sides together, place 1 medium blue print square on top of 1 navy **square**. Stitch ¼" from each side of drawn line (**Fig. 1**).

Fig. 1

2. Cut along drawn line. Open up and press to make 2 **Triangle-Squares**. Make 117 Triangle-squares.

Triangle-Squares (make 117)

3. Alternating medium blue fabrics, sew 4 **triangle-squares** and 1 medium blue small **triangle** together to make Unit 1. Make 13 Unit 1's.

Unit 1 (make 13)

61

4. Alternating medium blue fabrics, sew 5 **triangle-squares** and 1 medium blue small **triangle** together to make **Unit 2**. Make 13 Unit 2's.

Unit 2 (make 13)

5. Sew 1 **Unit 1** to 1 short side of 1 **medium triangle**. Sew 1 **Unit 2** to remaining short side of **medium triangle** to make **Unit 3**. Make 13 Unit 3's.

Unit 3 (make 13)

6. Sew 1 **Unit 3** to 1 navy **large triangle** to make **Block**. Make 13 Blocks.

Block (make 13)

ASSEMBLING THE QUILT TOP

Refer to the **Assembly Diagram** *for placement.*

1. Sew **Blocks** and **Side Setting Triangles** together in diagonal **Rows**.
2. Sew diagonal **Rows** together.
3. Sew **Corner Setting Triangles** to corners to complete Quilt Top.

FINISHING THE QUILT

1. Refer to **Quilting**, page 124, to mark, layer, and quilt. The Setting Triangles in Pat's quilt are machine quilted with large free-form feathers. The sky area has a sun and the water has dragonflies and swirls.
2. Refer to **Making A Hanging Sleeve**, page 126, to make and attach a hanging sleeve, if desired.
3. Use **binding strips** and follow **Making Straight-Grain Binding**, page 126, to make binding. Follow **Pat's Machine-Sewn Binding**, page 126, to bind quilt.

Assembly Diagram

Sheep's Feet

Tan sheep, cream sheep, brown sheep, and black sheep! The pastures and mountains of Ireland are home to thousands of cuddly sheep and how can you not fall in love with every single one of them?

Whether you're planning a trip, remembering a previous trip, or simply reading about Ireland, snuggle under this quick and cozy quilt and you'll soon be dreaming of sheep!

FABRIC REQUIREMENTS

Yardage is based on 43"/44" (109 cm/112 cm) wide fabric.

- 1¾ yds (1.6 m) of cream print #1 fabric
- 1¼ yds (1.1 m) of cream print #2 fabric
- ¼ yd (23 cm) **each** of 3 rust print fabrics
- ½ yd (46 cm) of 1 additional rust print fabric
- ¼ yd (23 cm) **each** of 3 brown print fabrics
- ½ yd (46 cm) of 1 additional brown print fabric
- 1 yd (91 cm) of black tone-on-tone print fabric
- ⅞ yd (80 cm) of black stripe fabric for inner border and binding
- 2⅜ yds (2.2 cm) of floral print fabric for outer border
- 7⅜ yds (6.7 cm) of fabric for backing

You will also need:
- 92" x 88" (234 cm x 224 cm) piece of batting

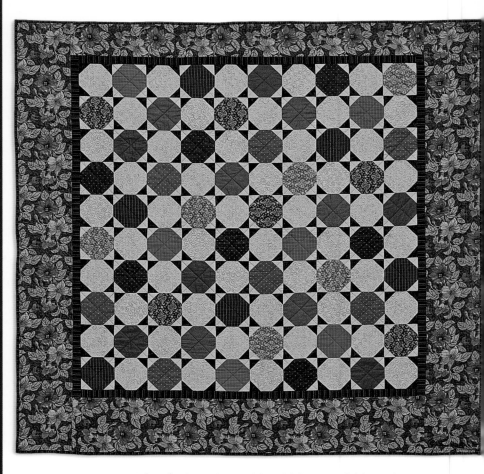

Finished Size: 84" x 80" (213 cm x 203 cm)
Finished Block Size: 6" x 6" (15 cm x 15 cm)

CUTTING THE PIECES

Refer to **Rotary Cutting**, *page 120, to cut fabrics. Cut all strips from the selvage-to-selvage width of the fabric unless otherwise noted. All measurements include ¼" seam allowances. Cutting lengths for borders include an extra 4" of length for "insurance." Borders will be trimmed to fit after measuring completed quilt top center.*

From cream print #1 fabric:
- Cut 6 strips 6½" wide. From these strips, cut 33 **large squares** 6½" x 6½".
- Cut 6 strips 2½" wide. From these strips, cut 96 **small squares** 2½" x 2½".

From cream print #2 fabric:
- Cut 3 strips 6½" wide. From these strips, cut 17 **large squares** 6½" x 6½".
- Cut 7 strips 2½" wide. From these strips, cut 104 **small squares** 2½" x 2½".

From *each* of 3 rust print fabrics:
- Cut 1 strip 6½" wide. From this strip, cut 6 **large squares** 6½" x 6½".

From additional rust print fabric:
- Cut 2 strips 6½" wide. From these strips, cut 7 **large squares** 6½" x 6½".

From *each* of 3 brown print fabrics:
- Cut 1 strip 6½" wide. From this strip, cut 6 **large squares** 6½" x 6½".

From 4th brown print fabric:
- Cut 2 strips 6½" wide. From these strips, cut 7 **large squares** 6½" x 6½".

From black tone-on-tone print fabric:
- Cut 13 strips 2½" wide. From these strips, cut 200 **small squares** 2½" x 2½".

From black stripe fabric:
- Cut 7 **inner border strips** 2" wide.
- Cut 9 **binding strips** 1¹/₂" wide.

From floral print fabric:
- Cut 2 *lengthwise* **side outer borders** 10¹/₂" x 83¹/₂".
- Cut 1 *lengthwise* **bottom outer border** 10¹/₂" x 67¹/₂".
- Cut 1 *lengthwise* **top outer border** 6¹/₂" x 67¹/₂".

MAKING THE BLOCKS

Follow **Piecing** *and* **Pressing**, *page 121, to assemble the blocks. Use* ¹/₄" *seam allowances throughout.*

1. Place one black **small square** on the upper left corner of one cream **large square** and stitch diagonally (**Fig. 1**). Trim ¹/₄" from stitching line (**Fig. 2**). Open up and press, pressing seam allowances toward darker fabric (**Fig. 3**).

Fig. 1	Fig. 2	Fig. 3

2. Place another black **small square** on the upper right corner of large square. Stitch, trim, and press as above. Continue adding black small squares to lower left and lower right corners to make **Block A**. Make 50 Block A's.

Block A (make 50)

3. Repeat **Steps 1–2** using cream **small squares** on corners of rust or brown **large squares** to make 50 **Block B's**.

Block B (make 50)

ASSEMBLING THE QUILT TOP CENTER

*Refer to the **Quilt Top Diagram**, for placement.*

1. Alternating Block's A and B, sew 10 blocks together to make a **Row**. Make 10 Rows.
2. Sew Rows together to make quilt top center.

ADDING THE BORDERS

1. Using diagonal seams (**Fig. 4**), sew **inner border strips** together end to end to make 1 continuous inner border.

Fig. 4

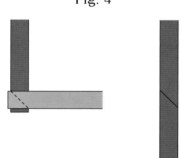

2. To determine length of top and bottom inner borders, measure **width** of quilt top center. From inner border strip, cut top and bottom inner borders the determined length. Matching centers and corners, sew borders to quilt top center. Press seam allowances toward borders.
3. To determine length of side inner borders, measure **length** of quilt top center (including added borders). From inner border strip, cut 2 side inner borders the determined length. Matching centers and corners, sew side inner borders to quilt top center. Press seam allowances toward borders.
4. Repeat **Steps 2-3** to sew outer borders to quilt.

FINISHING THE QUILT

1. Following **Quilting**, page 124, to mark, layer, and quilt as desired. Pat's quilt is machine quilted. The blocks with cream centers are quilted with squiggles to represent sheep's wool. Legs, a head, and a tail are quilted in the black corner triangles. The remaining blocks are quilted with a large X. There is a wavy line quilted in the inner border and a leaf pattern quilted in the outer border.
2. Follow **Making A Hanging Sleeve**, page 126, to make and attach a hanging sleeve, if desired.
3. Use **binding strips** and follow **Making Straight-Grain Binding**, page 126, to make binding. Follow **Pat's Machine-Sewn Binding**, page 126, to bind quilt.

Quilt Top Diagram

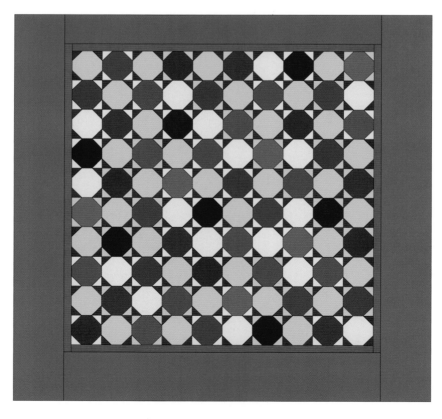

Pillowcase

Making pillowcases to match your bed-size quilt is a quick and easy way to add a decorator touch to any bedroom. Fabric requirements given are for one pillowcase.

Finished Size: 19³/₄" x 31" (50 cm x 79 cm)

FABRIC REQUIREMENTS

26¹/₂" x 40" (67 cm x 102 cm) piece of fabric for body of pillowcase

9³/₄" x 40" (25 cm x 102 cm) piece of fabric for band

1¹/₄" x 40" (3 cm x 102 cm) piece of fabric for trim

ASSEMBLING THE PILLOWCASE

Match right sides and raw edges and use ¹/₄" seam allowances throughout.

1. Matching short edges, fold body of pillowcase in half; pin. Sew along 1 long edge and 1 short edge. Turn body right side out; press.
2. Sew short ends of band together to make a loop.
3. Press 1 long edge of band ¹/₄" to wrong side.
4. Sew short ends of trim together to make a loop.
5. Sew 1 long edge of trim to unpressed edge of band. Press seam allowances toward band.
6. Sew remaining long edge of trim to body of pillowcase.
7. Fold pressed edge of band to inside of pillowcase until it covers the seam allowances between the trim and body of pillowcase; pin. Topstitch in place along edge of trim nearest body of pillowcase.
8. Press band flat.

With Needle and Thread

As quilters, the friendships we make often start with our common love of fabric and fibers. And, since all stitchers need a place to store their hand tools and supplies, wouldn't this cute little sewing case be the perfect project to make as a gift for your special quilting friends?

For me, this sewing case will serve as a reminder of my trip to Ireland and all my quilting friends, old and new, every time I use it!

Pat's Thoughts:
We had some "false alarms" for fabric shops, including one on the trip back from Cobh. We came to realize that "Quilt Centre" in Ireland meant finished home decorating goods. Jim volunteered to go inside to see if they had even a scrap of fabric to sell us. No fabric for us here, so we pushed on!

Jim's Travel Tip:
Before leaving home, notify your credit card company that you are traveling to Ireland. They will allow your charges to go through and won't think someone has stolen your card.

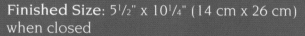

Finished Size: 5¹/₂" x 10¹/₄" (14 cm x 26 cm) when closed

FABRIC REQUIREMENTS

Yardage is based on 43"/44" (109 cm/112 cm) wide fabric

- 13" x 13" (33 cm x 33 cm) square **each** of 2 tan print fabrics
- 12" x 13" (30 cm x 33 cm) piece of fabric for large pocket
- 6" x 6" (15 cm x 15 cm) piece of red wool fabric for small pocket and appliqués
- 6" x 8" (15 cm x 20 cm) piece of green wool fabric for appliqués
- 1 fat quarter* of brown print fabric for binding and closure

You will also need:

- 13" x 13" (33 cm x 33 cm) square of batting
- Paper-backed fusible web
- Tissue paper
- Assorted buttons — 5 green and 10 red
- Black #8 pearl cotton
- 3 sew-on snaps
- Water-soluble fabric marking pen

*A fat quarter = approximately 18" x 20" (46 cm x 51 cm).

CUTTING THE PIECES

Follow **Rotary Cutting***, page 120, to cut fabric. All measurements include* ¹/₄" *seam allowances.*

From fabric for large pocket:
- Cut 2 **large pockets** 5" x 12".

From red wool fabric:
- Use pattern, page 74, to cut 1 **small pocket**.

From brown print fabric:
- Cut 1" x 40" **bias strip** for binding, pieced as needed.
- Cut 2 **closure squares** 2¹/₂" x 2¹/₂" for closure.

CUTTING THE APPLIQUES

Patterns, page 74, are reversed and do not include seam allowances. Follow **Preparing Fusible Appliqués***, page 122, to cut appliqués.*

From red wool fabric:
- Cut 2 **spool ends** (C)

From green wool fabric:
- Cut 1 **shamrock** (A)
- Cut 1 **spool of thread** (B)

ASSEMBLING THE SEWING CASE

Refer to the photos, page 72, for placement. Note placement of appliquéd and embroidered details and pockets in relation to closure. Use black pearl cotton for all embroidery.

1. Layer 1 **tan print square** (wrong side up), **batting**, and remaining **tan print square** (right side up). Follow **Quilting**, page 124, to quilt square in $1^1/4$" diagonal crosshatch quilting.

2. Use sewing case pattern, page 75, to cut sewing case from quilted square.

3. Decide which side will be outside of sewing case. Match center tops and fold sewing case in half. Mark the fold line with pins.

4. For large pocket, match right sides and raw edges of **large pockets** and sew along each long edge of pocket. Turn the pocket right sides out; press.

5. Aligning 1 long edge of the pocket with the fold line of the sewing case, position the pocket on the inside of the sewing case. Topstitch pocket in place along long edge at fold line. Trim side edges of pocket even with curved edges of sewing case. Baste pocket in place along curved edges.

6. To bind raw edge, press 1 long edge and 1 short end of **bias strip** $1/4$" to wrong side. Matching right sides and raw edges and beginning with unpressed end, pin unpressed edge of bias strip to sewing case. Sew bias strip to sewing case using a $1/4$" seam allowance. Fold bias strip to inside of sewing case and Blind Stitch, page 128, folded edge to sewing case covering stitching line.

7. Matching right sides and raw edges, sew the two **closure squares** together, leaving an opening for turning. Trim corners and turn the closure right sides out; press.

8. Fold the sewing case closed. Position the closure at the center so it just fits over the edges of the sewing case; pin.

9. On the back, topstitch the closure to the sewing case. On the front, sew a snap under the closure through the top layer of fabric only.

10. Position **small pocket** on inside of sewing case below the large pocket; pin. Do not attach at this time. Use fabric-marking pen to draw the words. Remove the small pocket. Use a **Stem Stitch**, page 128, to embroider the words.

11. Fuse shamrock (A) to the small pocket. Refer to **Blanket Stitch**, page 128, to sew the shamrock to the small pocket. Stack buttons and sew to shamrock.

12. Blanket Stitch the top edge of the small pocket from mark "x" to mark "x". Blanket Stitch the remaining edge to the inside of the sewing case through the top layer of fabric only. Sew a snap under the pocket opening.

13. Fuse appliqués **B** and **C** on outside of sewing case. Blanket Stitch the appliqués to the sewing case through top layer of fabric only.

14. Use fabric-marking pen to draw stems and words around appliqués. Embroider the stems and words through top layer of fabric only using a Stem Stitch.

15. Sew buttons to ends of stems. Stack two buttons and sew to center of spool.

16. Stack buttons and sew to top edge of large pocket. Sew a snap under the pocket opening.

As we left Avoca all traffic came to a halt to allow a bicycle race to pass! What fun!

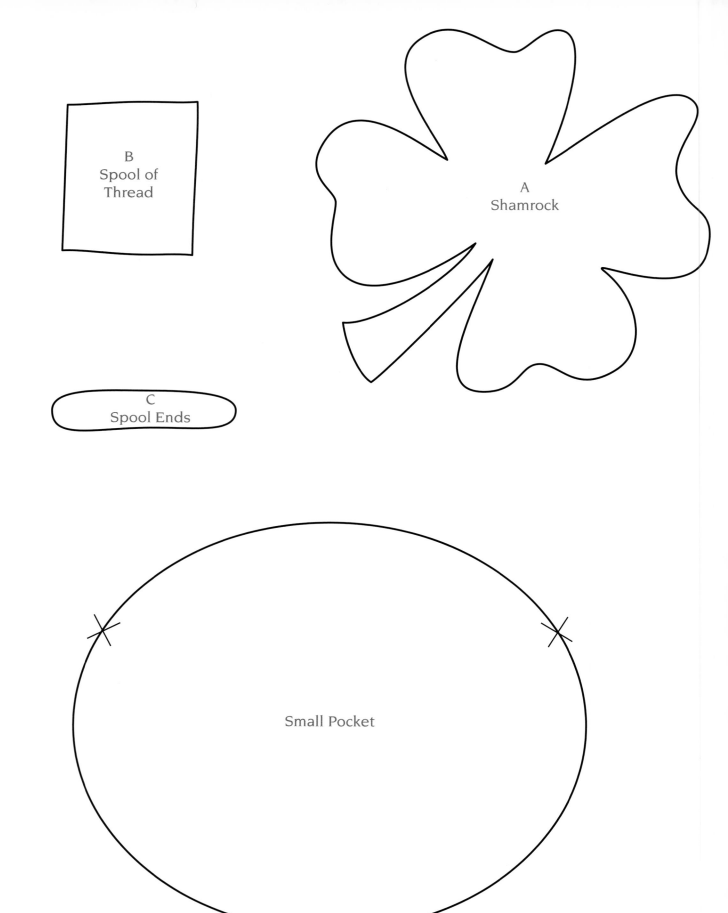

B
Spool of
Thread

A
Shamrock

C
Spool Ends

Small Pocket

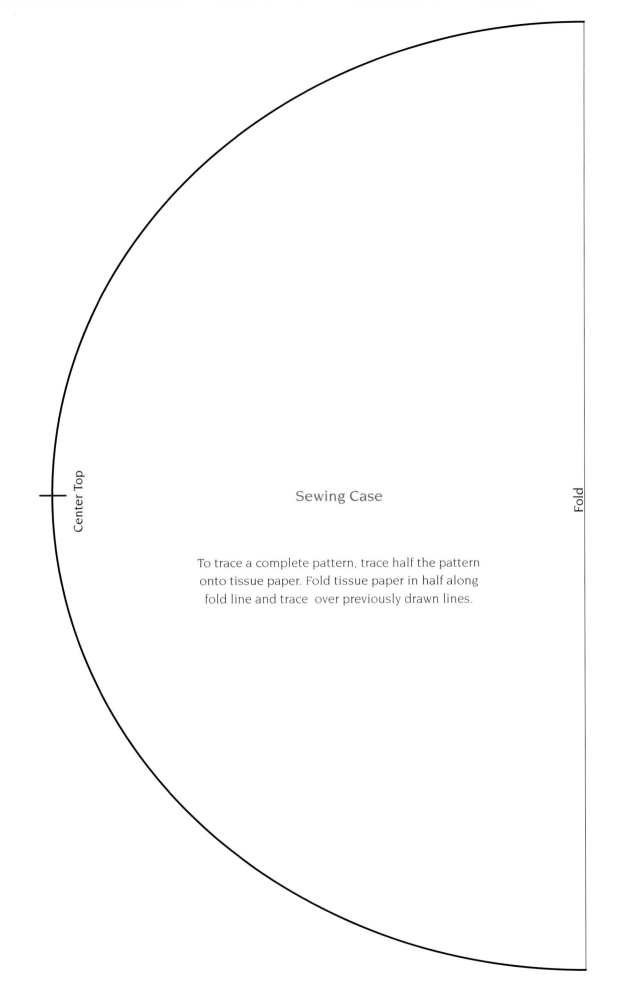

Center Top

Fold

Sewing Case

To trace a complete pattern, trace half the pattern
onto tissue paper. Fold tissue paper in half along
fold line and trace over previously drawn lines.

Luck of the Irish Wall Hanging

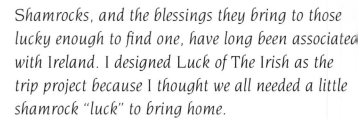

Shamrocks, and the blessings they bring to those lucky enough to find one, have long been associated with Ireland. I designed Luck of The Irish as the trip project because I thought we all needed a little shamrock "luck" to bring home.

This wall hanging features my easy Running Stitch method of Needleturn Appliqué. To add a little bling I choose to embellish my wall hanging with beads.

The group members were so excited about this project that some of them cut (can you believe it?) and stitched on the bus as we toured.

Turn to page 82 to see this versatile design used in horizontal format as a table runner.

*May your blessings outnumber the shamrocks that grow.
And may trouble avoid you, wherever you go*

Finished Size: 15" x 40" (38 cm x 102 cm)

FABRIC REQUIREMENTS

Yardage is based on 43"/44" (109 cm/112 cm) wide fabric.

- ³/₈ yd (34 cm) of yellow print fabric
- ¹/₂ yd (46 cm) of blue print fabric for border and binding
- 4¹/₂" x 11¹/₂" (11 cm x 29 cm) piece of red print fabric for appliqués.
- 12¹/₂" x 4³/₄" (32 cm x 12 cm) piece of blue print fabric for appliqués
- ¹/₂ yd (46 cm) of green print #1 fabric for appliqués
- 6" x 11" (15 cm x 28 cm) piece of green print #2 fabric for appliqués
- 5" x 9" (13 cm x 23 cm) piece of green stripe fabric for appliqués
- 1¹/₄ yds (1.1 m) of fabric for backing

You will also need:

- 19" x 44" (48 cm x 112 cm) piece of batting
- Template plastic
- Permanent fine-point pen
- Water- or air-soluble fabric marking pen
- Variegated embroidery floss or #5 pearl cotton
- Assorted beads (optional)

CUTTING THE PIECES

Follow **Rotary Cutting**, *page 120, to cut fabric. Cut all strips from the selvage-to-selvage width of the fabric. All measurements include* ¼" *seam allowances.*

From yellow print fabric:
- Cut **background rectangle** 10½" x 35½".

From blue print fabric:
- Cut 2 **side borders** 2½" x 35½".
- Cut 2 **top/bottom borders** 2½" x 14½".
- Cut 4 **binding strips** 1½" wide.

From green print #1 fabric:
- Cut 1 **bias strip for stems** 1" x 45", pieced as necessary.

CUTTING THE APPLIQUÉS

Patterns on pages 80 and 81 do not include seam allowances. Refer to **Template Cutting**, *page 121, to cut appliqués.*

From blue print fabric:
- Cut 1 **bowl** (**D**).

From red print fabric:
- Cut 1 **bowl trim** (**E**).
- Cut 4 **stars** (**K**).

From green print #1 fabric:
- Cut 4 **shamrocks** (**H**).
- Cut 4 **stems** (**F**).

From green print #2 fabric:
- Cut 1 **shamrock** (**I**).
- Cut 1 **stem** (**G**).

From green stripe fabric:
- Cut 3 **leaves**; cut 1 **leaf** in reverse (**J**).

ASSEMBLING THE WALL HANGING TOP

Use ¼" *seam allowances throughout.*

1. Sew the **side borders** to **background rectangle**.
2. Sew the **top/bottom borders** to **background rectangle** to make **wall hanging top**.

ADDING THE APPLIQUÉS

In this hand appliqué method, the needle is used to turn the seam allowance under as you sew the appliqué to the background fabric using a Running Stitch.

1. Matching wrong sides, fold **bias strip for stems** in half lengthwise; do not press. Stitch along length of strip ½" from fold. Trim seam allowances to approximately ⅟₁₆". Centering seam on back of strip, press bias strip flat. Cut two 4" lengths (**A**), two 6" lengths (**B**), and one 21" length (**C**).
2. Arrange stems on wall hanging top; pin or hand baste in place.
3. Arrange appliqués on wall hanging top in alphabetical order and pin in place.
4. Thread a straw or appliqué needle with a single strand of general-purpose sewing thread the color of the appliqué; knot one end.
5. To appliqué pressed bias strips, use a **Running Stitch,** page 128, to sew along edges.
6. For appliqués, begin on as straight an edge as possible and use point of needle to turn under a small amount of seam allowance, concealing drawn line on appliqué. Use a Running Stitch to sew the appliqué to the wall hanging top, stitching along the edge of the appliqué.
7. To stitch outward points, stitch to ½" from point (**Fig. 1**). Turn seam allowance under at point (**Fig. 2**); then turn remainder of seam allowance between stitching and point. Stitch to point. Turn under small amount of seam allowance past point and resume stitching.

Fig. 1

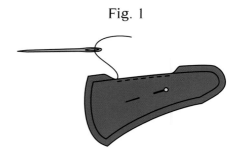

Fig. 2

8. To stitch inward point, stitch to ½" from point (**Fig. 3**). Clip to but not through seam allowance at point (**Fig. 4**). Turn seam allowance under between stitching and point. Stitch to point. Turn under small amount of seam allowance past point and resume stitching.

Fig. 3   Fig. 4

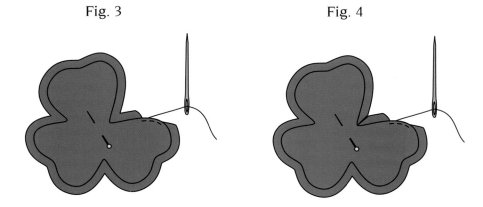

9. Do not turn under or stitch seam allowances that will be covered by other appliqué pieces.

FINISHING THE WALL HANGING

1. Use fabric marking pen to write words onto wall hanging top. Use embroidery floss or pearl cotton to stitch the words using a **Stem Stitch**, page 128.
2. Refer to **Quilting**, page 124, to mark, layer, and quilt as desired. Pat's wall hanging is quilted in the ditch around each applique and border. The background is meandered quilted. There are veins quilted in the shamrocks and wavy horizontal lines in the bowl.
3. Refer to **Making A Hanging Sleeve**, page 126, to make and attach a hanging sleeve, if desired.
4. Use **binding strips** and follow **Making Straight-Grain Binding**, page 126, to make binding. Follow **Pat's Machine-Sewn Binding**, page 126, to bind wall hanging.
5. Sew beads to appliqués as desired.

Jim's Travel Tip:
Before leaving your hotel to explore, be sure you have a business card or brochure with the hotel's address and telephone number. In the event you get lost, you can ask someone for directions or tell a taxi driver where your hotel is located.

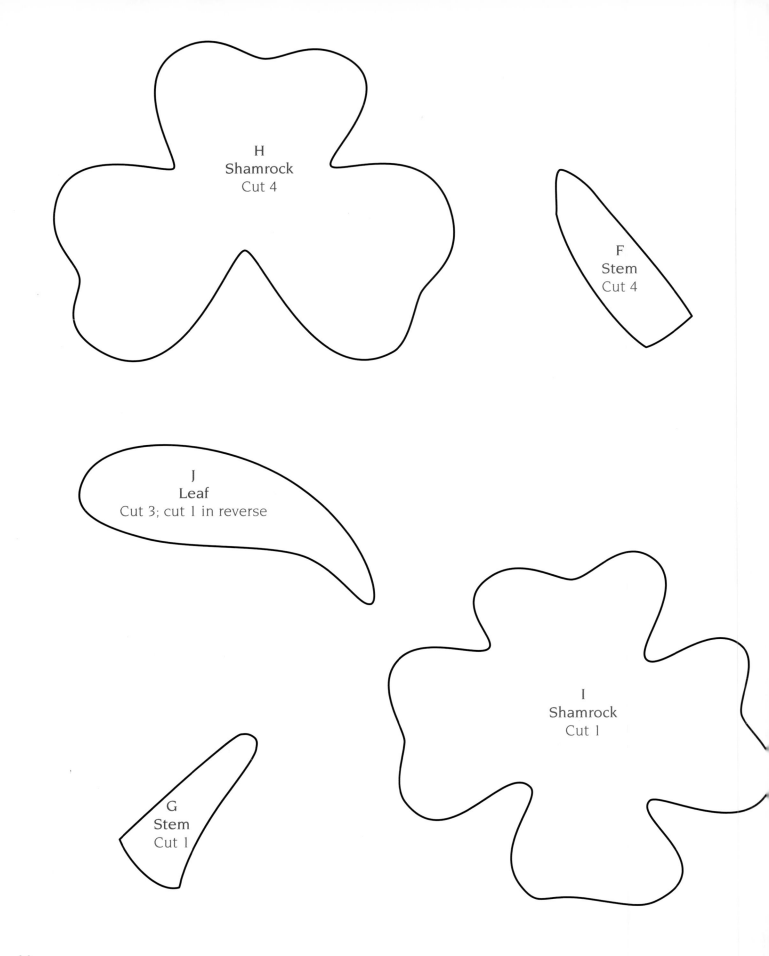

H
Shamrock
Cut 4

F
Stem
Cut 4

J
Leaf
Cut 3; cut 1 in reverse

G
Stem
Cut 1

I
Shamrock
Cut 1

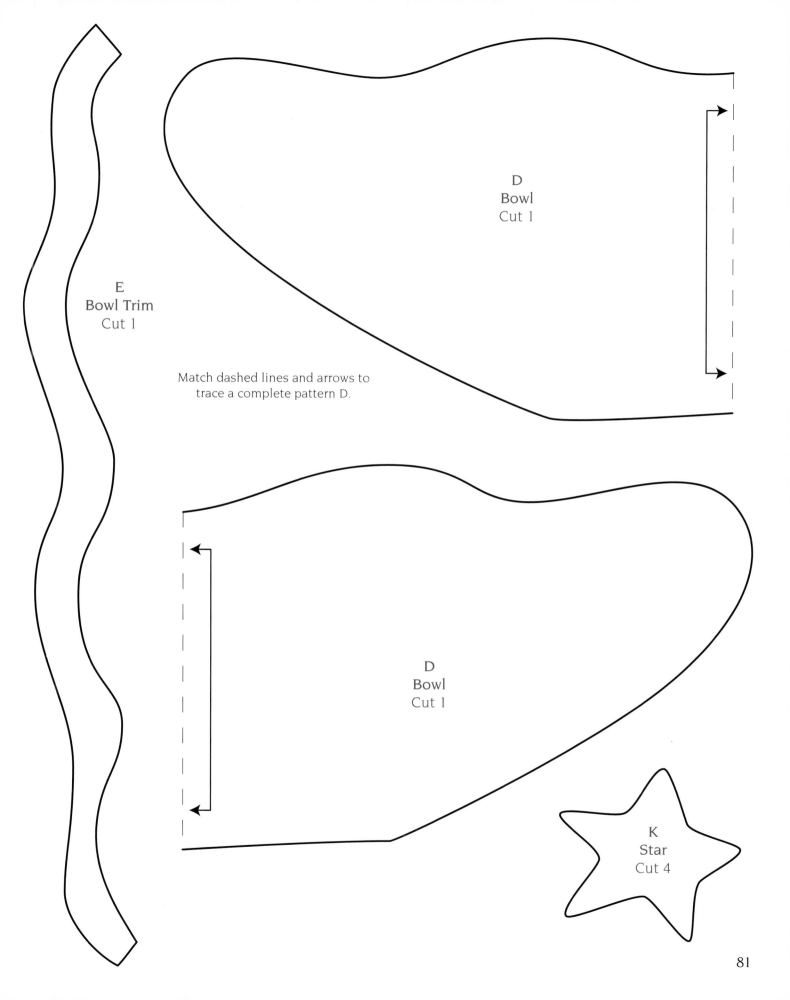

E
Bowl Trim
Cut 1

D
Bowl
Cut 1

Match dashed lines and arrows to trace a complete pattern D.

D
Bowl
Cut 1

K
Star
Cut 4

Luck of the Irish Table Runner

In Ireland at breakfast each day we dined at tables set with pretty teapots and chose from an array of taste-tempting baked goods and fresh fruit. To bring a little bit of the Irish breakfast feel to your table, whip up one of these delightful runners then sit back and enjoy some scones and a cup of tea!

To make it extra fast and easy, this version of Luck of the Irish features fusible appliqué and Machine Blanket Stitch.

Because both the table runner and the wall hanging, shown on page 76, are so much fun to make you may want to stitch one of each for "double the luck"!

Jim's Travel Tip:
A versatile item to have is a backpack. Use it as a carry-on for the airplane, to hold cameras, maps, and jackets on day trips, and for stowing small packages when shopping.

Jim's Travel Tip:
Before checking out of your hotel room, it's a nice gesture to leave the cleaning crew a tip and maybe even a thank you note. It is appreciated more than you can imagine.

Finished Size: 40" x 15" (102 cm x 38 cm)

FABRIC REQUIREMENTS

Yardage is based on 43"/44" (109 cm/112 cm) wide fabric.

⅜ yd (34 cm) of yellow print fabric

½ yd (46 cm) of blue print fabric for border and binding

3½" x 11½" (9 cm x 29 cm) piece of red print fabric for appliqués

12½" x 4¾" (32 cm x 12 cm) piece of blue print fabric for appliqués

½ yd (46 cm) of green print #1 fabric for appliqués

4½" x 9" (11 cm x 23 cm) piece of green print #2 fabric for appliqués

5" x 10" (13 cm x 25 cm) piece of green stripe fabric for appliqués

1¼ yds (1.1 m) of fabric for backing

You will also need:

19" x 44" (48 cm x 112 cm) piece of batting

Paper-backed fusible web

Stabilizer or spray starch

CUTTING THE PIECES

Follow **Rotary Cutting**, *page 120, to cut fabric. Cut all strips from the selvage-to-selvage width of the fabric. All measurements include ¼" seam allowances.*

From yellow print fabric:

- Cut **background rectangle** 10½" x 35½".

From blue print fabric:

- Cut 2 **top/bottom borders** 2½" x 35½".
- Cut 2 **side borders** 2½" x 14½".
- Cut 4 **binding strips** 1½" wide.

From green print #1 fabric:

- Cut 1 **bias strip for stems** 1" x 45", pieced as necessary.

CUTTING THE APPLIQUÉS

Patterns, pages 86 and 87, are reversed and do not include seam allowances. Follow **Preparing Fusible Appliqués**, *page 122, to cut appliqués.*

From blue print fabric:

- Cut bowl (**D**).

From red print fabric:

- Cut 1 bowl trim (**E**).
- Cut 4 stars (**H**).

From green print #1 fabric:
- Cut 2 shamrocks (**F**).

From green print #2 fabric:
- Cut 2 shamrocks (**F**).
- Cut 1 shamrock (**G**).

From green stripe fabric:
- Cut 3 leaves; cut 3 leaves in reverse (**I**).

ASSEMBLING THE TABLE RUNNER

Use ¼ seam allowances throughout.

1. Sew the **top/bottom borders** to **background rectangle**.
2. Sew the **side borders** to background rectangle to make table runner top.

ADDING THE APPLIQUÉS

*Refer to **Machine Blanket Stitch Appliqué**, page 122, for technique.*

1. Matching wrong sides, fold **bias strip for stems** in half lengthwise; do not press. Stitch along length of strip ½" from fold. Trim seam allowances to approximately ¹⁄₁₆". Centering seam on back of strip, press bias strip flat. Cut four 3½" lengths (**A**), two 7" lengths (**B**), and two 11" lengths (**C**).
2. Arrange stems on table runner top; pin or hand baste in place.
3. Arrange appliqués on background rectangle working from background to forefront in alphabetical order; fuse in place.
4. Machine Blanket Stitch Appliqué pieces to table runner top.

FINISHING THE TABLE RUNNER

1. Refer to **Quilting**, page 124, to mark, layer, and quilt as desired. Pat's table runner is quilted with outline quilting around the appliqués, wavy horizontal lines on the bowl, veins in the leaves and hearts in the shamrocks. There are meandering leaves and swirls in the background and hearts and feathers in the borders.
2. Use **binding strips** and follow **Making Straight-Grain Binding**, page 126, to make binding. Follow **Pat's Machine-Sewn Binding**, page 126, to bind table runner.

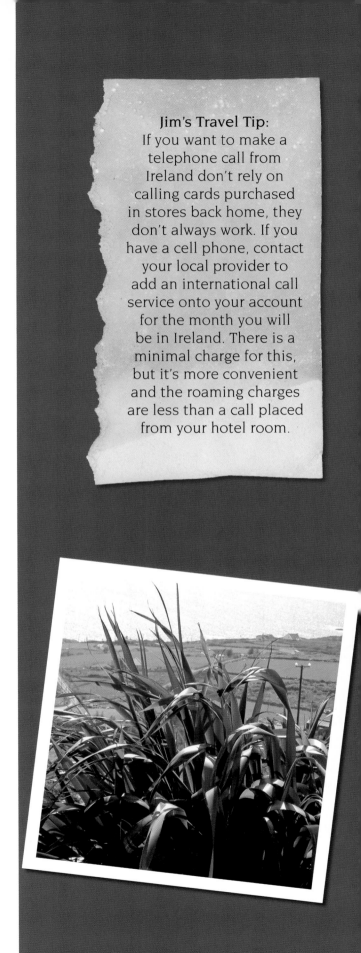

Jim's Travel Tip:
If you want to make a telephone call from Ireland don't rely on calling cards purchased in stores back home, they don't always work. If you have a cell phone, contact your local provider to add an international call service onto your account for the month you will be in Ireland. There is a minimal charge for this, but it's more convenient and the roaming charges are less than a call placed from your hotel room.

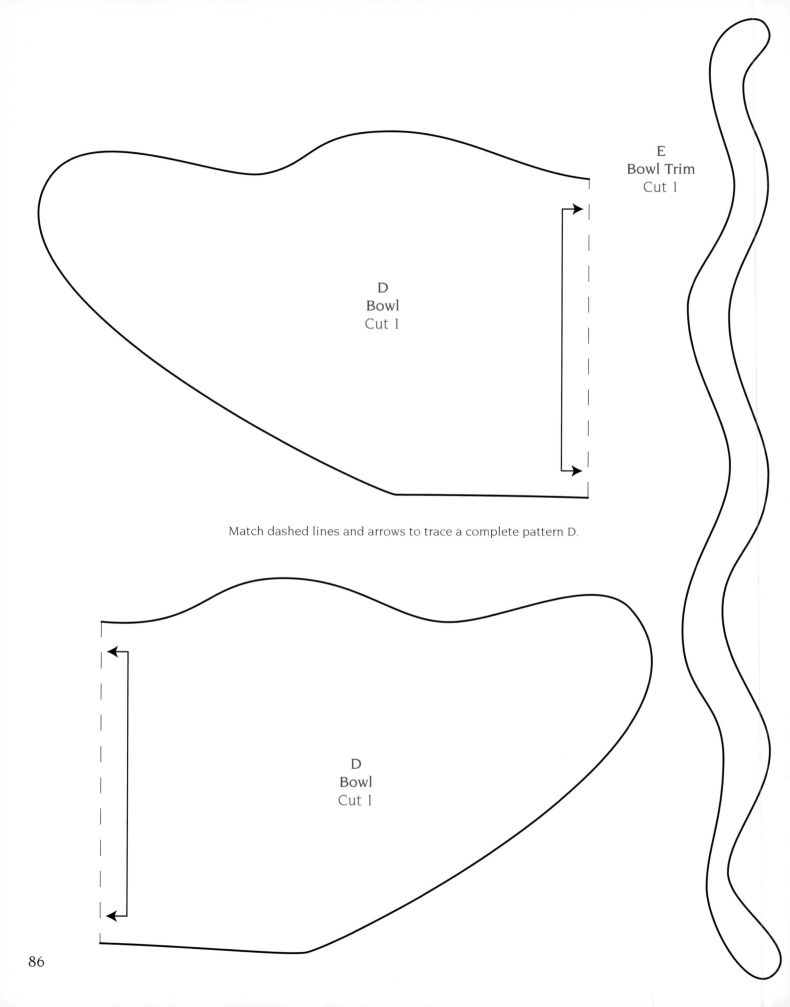

E
Bowl Trim
Cut 1

D
Bowl
Cut 1

Match dashed lines and arrows to trace a complete pattern D.

D
Bowl
Cut 1

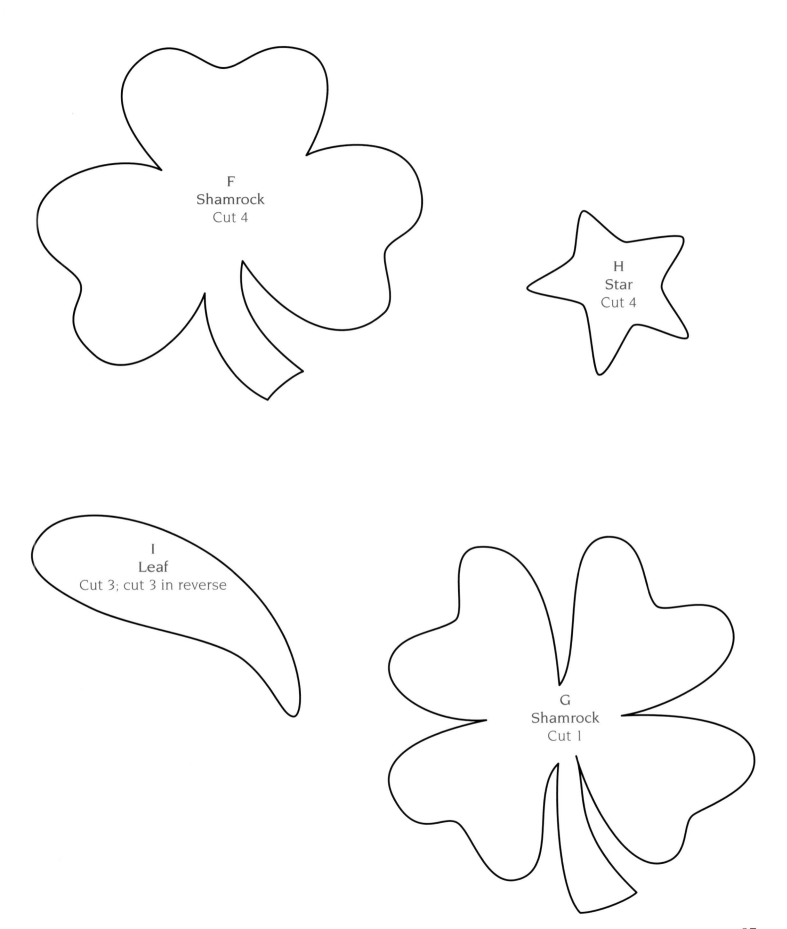

F
Shamrock
Cut 4

H
Star
Cut 4

I
Leaf
Cut 3; cut 3 in reverse

G
Shamrock
Cut 1

One of my goals is to have a different quilt for each month of the year. How fitting after my trip to Ireland to make a Shamrock quilt to sleep under in March!

While designing this quilt, I came across some interesting bits of shamrock trivia. The name "shamrock" derives from the Irish word, seamrog, which translates to "little clover."

According to Irish legend, the missionary, Saint Patrick, demonstrated the principle behind the Trinity using a three-leaf shamrock.

The leaves of four-leaf shamrocks are sometimes said to stand for faith, hope, love, and luck.

On average, there are 10,000 three-leaf shamrocks for every instance of a true four-leaf shamrock; we are lucky if we find one!

When making the appliqué blocks for this quilt, you can choose how many blocks you want to have three and how many you want to have four-leaf shamrocks. Wouldn't it be fun to make just one of the twenty-four blocks a four-leaf shamrock and let people "find" the lucky shamrock in your quilt!

Dreaming of Shamrocks

Finished Size: 87" x 83" (221 cm x 211 cm)
Finished Block Size: 9" x 9" (23 cm x 23 cm)

FABRIC REQUIREMENTS
Yardage is based on 43"/44" (109 cm/112 cm) wide fabric.

- 1¾ yds (1.6 m) of cream print fabric
- 1 yd (91 cm) of large black floral print fabric
- 2½ yds (2.3 m) of small black floral print fabric
- ⅞ yd (80 cm) of red print fabric for inner border and binding
- ½ yd (46 cm) **each** of 6 different green print fabrics - green prints #1- #6
- 1⅜ yds (1.3 m) of green print #7 fabric
- ¼ yd (23 cm) of blue print fabric
- 7⅝ yds (7 m) of fabric for backing

You will also need:
- 95" x 91" (241 cm x 231 cm) piece of batting
- Paper-backed fusible web
- Stabilizer or spray starch
- Square acrylic ruler (at least 12" x 12")

Jim's Travel Tip:
If you have an overnight flight to Ireland, do not go to sleep until 9pm or later on the day you arrive. If you take a nap in the afternoon, it is likely you will be awake at 2am the following morning.

Jim's Travel Tip:
If you are touring the southwest part of Ireland, you will probably tour the Ring of Kerry or the Dingle Peninsula. Using a neck or back pillow for your comfort on these long bus rides is a good idea. And, if you are afraid of heights you may wish to avoid a window seat, as the cliffs are steep and high.

CUTTING THE PIECES

Follow **Rotary Cutting***, page 120, to cut fabric. Cut all strips from the selvage-to-selvage width of the fabric unless otherwise noted. All measurements include ¼" seam allowances. Cutting lengths for borders include an extra 4" of length for "insurance." Borders will be trimmed to fit after measuring completed quilt top center.*

From cream print fabric:
- Cut 6 strips 9½" wide. From these strips, cut 24 **large squares** 9½" x 9½".

From large black floral print fabric:
- Cut 5 strips 6" wide. From these strips, cut 25 **small squares** 6" x 6".

From small black floral print fabric:
- Cut 2 *lengthwise* **side borders** 10½" x 86½".
- Cut 1 *lengthwise* **bottom border** 10½" x 70½".
- Cut 1 *lengthwise* **top border** 6½" x 70½".

From red print fabric:
- Cut 7 **inner border strips** 2" wide.
- Cut 9 **binding strips** 1½" wide.

From *each* of 4 green print fabrics:
- Cut 2 strips 6½" wide. From these strips, cut 8 squares 6½" x 6½". Cut each square **once** diagonally to make 4 sets of 4 **triangles**.

From *each* of 3 green print fabrics:
- Cut 1 strip 6½" wide. From this strip, cut 6 squares 6½" x 6½". Cut each square **once** diagonally to make 3 sets of 4 **triangles**.

CUTTING THE APPLIQUES

Patterns on pages 94 and 95 are reversed and do not include seam allowances. Follow **Preparing Fusible Appliqués***, page 122, to cut appliqués.*

From *each* of 4 green print fabrics (1-4):
- Cut 3 shamrocks (**A** or **B**).

From *each* of 2 green print fabrics (5 and 6):
- Cut 4 shamrocks (**A** or **B**).

From green print fabric (7):
- Cut 4 shamrocks (**A** or **B**).
- Cut 18 swags (**C**).

From blue print fabric:
- Cut 19 dots (**D**).

MAKING THE BLOCKS

Refer to **Piecing** *and* **Pressing***, page 121, to assemble blocks. Use ¼" seam allowances throughout.*

Diamond Blocks

Note: *For each block, use 4 matching triangles.*

1. Fold each **small square** in half each way and finger press a crease in both directions.
2. Matching narrow points, fold each **triangle** and finger press a crease.
3. Matching creases, sew 1 triangle to opposite sides of 1 small square (**Fig. 1**).

Fig. 1

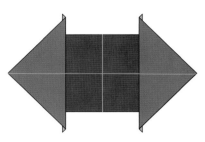

4. Trim the excess points even with the small square (**Fig. 2**).

Fig. 2

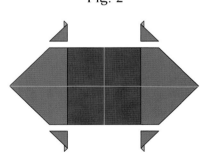

5. Matching creases, sew a triangle to each remaining side of small square (**Fig. 3**).

Fig. 3

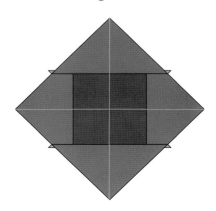

6. To trim the block to 9½" x 9½", line up a square ruler so the 4¾" line (shown in red) is down the center of the diamond. Trim the right edge (**Fig. 4**).

Fig. 4

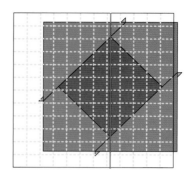

7. Turn the trimmed block ½ turn to the opposite edge. Repeat **Step 6** to trim opposite edge.
8. Repeat Steps 6-7 to trim remaining edges to make **Diamond Block**. Make 25 Diamond Blocks.

Diamond Block (make 25)

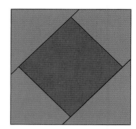

Shamrock Blocks

*Refer to **Machine Blanket Stitch Appliqué**, page 122, for technique.*

1. Arrange 1 shamrock appliqué (**A** or **B**) on each **large square**; fuse.
2. Machine Blanket Stitch Appliqué shamrocks to large squares to make **Shamrock Blocks**. Make 24 Shamrock Blocks.

ASSEMBLING THE QUILT TOP CENTER

*Refer to the **photo**, page 90, for placement.*

1. Alternating blocks, sew 4 Diamond Blocks and 3 Shamrock Blocks together to make **Row A**. Make 4 Row A's.
2. Alternating blocks, sew 4 Shamrock Blocks and 3 Diamond Blocks together to make **Row B**. Make 3 Row B's.
3. Sew Row A's and Row B's together to make quilt top center.

ADDING THE BORDERS

1. Using diagonal seams (**Fig. 5**), sew **inner border strips** together end to end to make 1 continuous inner border strip.

Fig. 5

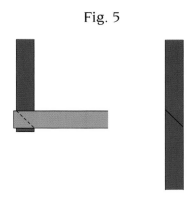

2. To determine length of top/bottom inner borders, measure **width** of quilt top center. From inner border strip, cut 2 **top/bottom inner borders** the determined length. Matching centers and corners, sew top/bottom inner borders to quilt top center. Press seam allowances toward borders.
3. To determine length of side inner borders, measure **length** (including added borders) of quilt top center. From inner border strip, cut 2 **side inner borders** the determined length. Matching centers and corners, sew side inner borders to quilt top center. Press seam allowances toward borders.
4. Repeat **Steps 2-3** to add outer borders.

Instructions for making coordinating pillowcases can be found on page 69

ADDING APPLIQUÉS TO THE BORDER

*Refer to **Machine Blanket Stitch Appliqué**, page 122, for technique.*

1. Arrange 6 swags (**C**) on side and bottom borders with the tips touching or slightly overlapping. Adjust swags to fit across the borders. Fuse swags in place.
2. Machine Blanket Stitch Appliqué swags to borders.
3. Arrange dots (**D**) at end of each swag; fuse.
4. Machine Blanket Stitch Appliqué dots to borders.

FINISHING THE QUILT

1. Following **Quilting**, page 124, to mark, layer, and quilt as desired. Pat's quilt is quilted in the ditch around the diamonds. There are swirls in the diamonds and hearts in the triangles of each Diamond Block and echo quilting in each Shamrock Block. There is a wavy line quilted in the inner border and the scallops. The outer border is quilted with lines echoing the swags.
2. Refer to **Making a Hanging Sleeve**, page 126, to make and attach a hanging sleeve, if desired.
3. Use binding strips and follow **Making Straight-Grain Binding**, page 126, to make binding. Follow **Pat's Machine-Sewn Binding**, page 126, to bind quilt.

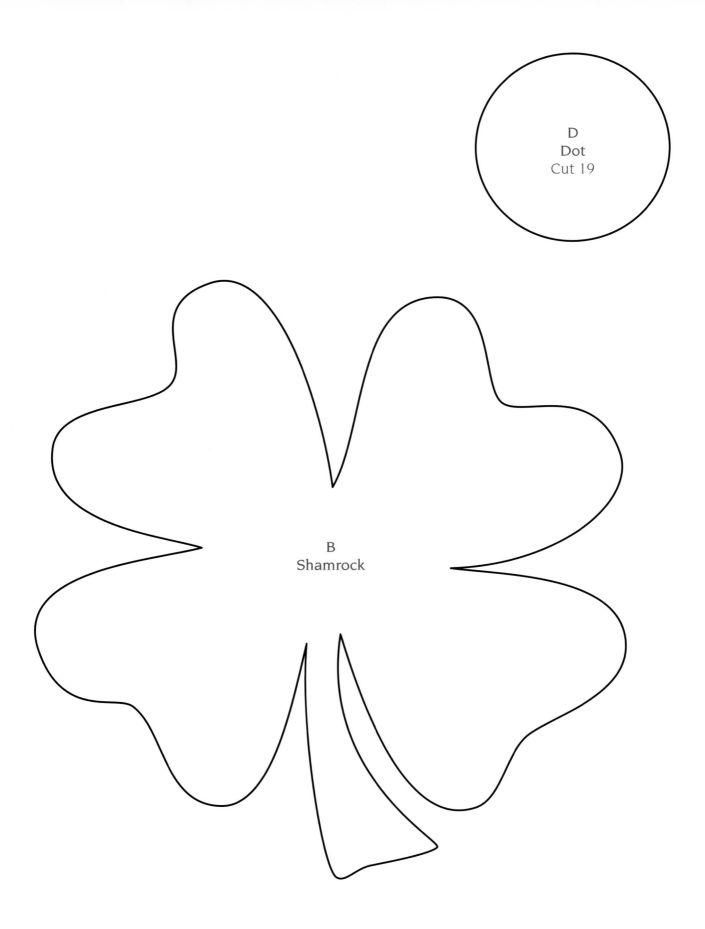

D
Dot
Cut 19

B
Shamrock

C
Swag
Cut 18

A
Shamrock

Sheep on the Mountain

For me, one of the highlights of the trip was our stop at Kells Sheep Centre. Brendan's talk about the various types of sheep was fascinating. I never realized there are so many different breeds of sheep!

The sheep herding demonstration was amazing. And, what fun to see the sheep up close since they are usually very timid and don't allow people to get near them.

The whole experience was so educational and entertaining! For the remainder of the trip we were constantly watching for sheep on the mountains!

Finished Size: 19" x 44" (48 cm x 112 cm)

FABRIC REQUIREMENTS

Yardage is based on 43"/44" (109 cm/112 cm) wide fabric.

$\frac{1}{2}$ yd (46 cm) of cream print for background

$\frac{3}{8}$ yd (34 cm) of black print #1 for borders

$\frac{1}{4}$ yd (23 cm) of black print #2 for binding and faces

12$\frac{1}{2}$" x 13" (32 cm x 33 cm) piece of green print #1 for upper hill

12$\frac{1}{2}$" x 12" (32 cm x 30 cm) piece of green print #2 for middle hill

12$\frac{1}{2}$" x 15$\frac{1}{2}$" (32 cm x 39 cm) piece of green print #3 for lower hill

4" x 8" (10 cm x 20 cm) piece **each** of 2 red prints for stars and houses

5" x 9" (13 cm x 23 cm) piece of yellow print #1 for roofs

2" x 3" (5 cm x 8 cm) piece of yellow print #2 for doors

5" x 5" (13 cm x 13 cm) piece **each** of 3 tan prints for sheep

3" x 3" (8 cm x 8 cm) piece of light brown print for legs

1$\frac{3}{8}$ yds (1.3 m) of fabric for backing

You will also need:

23" x 48" (58 cm x 122 cm) piece of batting

Paper-backed fusible web

Stabilizer or spray starch

CUTTING THE PIECES

Follow **Rotary Cutting**, *page 120, to cut fabric. Cut all strips from the selvage-to-selvage width of the fabric. All measurements include* ¹⁄₄" *seam allowances.*
From cream print fabric:
- Cut 1 **rectangle** 12¹⁄₂" x 37¹⁄₂".

From black print #1:
- Cut 2 **side borders** 3¹⁄₂" x 37¹⁄₂".
- Cut 2 **top/bottom borders** 3¹⁄₂" x 18¹⁄₂".

From black print #2:
- Cut 4 **binding strips** 1¹⁄₂" wide.

CUTTING THE APPLIQUÉS

Appliqué patterns A-G on pages 100 and 101 are reversed and do not include seam allowances. Follow **Preparing Fusible Appliqués**, *page 122, to cut appliqués.*
From red print #1:
- Cut 3 stars (**A**).

From red print #2:
- Cut 3 houses (**B**).

From yellow print #1:
- Cut 3 roofs (**C**).

From yellow print #2:
- Cut 3 doors (**D**).

From *each* tan print:
- Cut 1 sheep (**F**).

From light brown print:
- Cut 6 legs; cut 6 legs in reverse (**E**).

From black print #2:
- Cut 3 faces (**G**).

ASSEMBLING THE QUILT TOP

Follow **Piecing** and **Pressing**, *page 121,* and **Machine Blanket Stitch Appliqué**, *page 122, to make quilt top. Refer to* **Wall Hanging Top Diagram**, *page 100, for placement. Use* ¹⁄₄" *seam allowances throughout.*

1. Trace hill pattern, page 101, onto tracing paper; cut out.
2. Referring to **Hill Diagrams** and aligning side edges of pattern with side edges of rectangle, use hill pattern to mark, then trim curved top edge of **upper hill**, **middle hill** (reversed), and **lower hill rectangles**. Follow measurements to trim bottom edges of hill rectangles.
3. With right sides facing up and matching bottom and side edges, place lower hill on **background rectangle**.
4. Matching side edges, tuck bottom edge of middle hill under top edge of lower hill.
5. Matching side edges, tuck bottom edge of upper hill under top edge of middle hill.
6. Machine Blanket Stitch Appliqué top edge of each hill to background rectangle.
7. Sew **side** then **top/bottom borders** to background rectangle to make wall hanging top.

Hill Diagrams

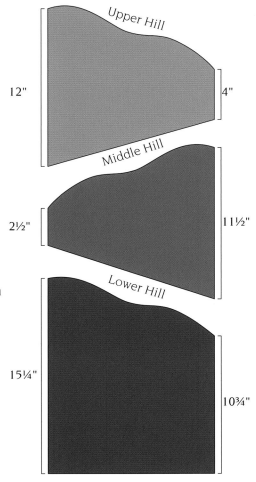

Upper Hill — 12", 4"

Middle Hill — 2¹⁄₂", 11¹⁄₂"

Lower Hill — 15¹⁄₄", 10¾"

Jim's Travel Tip:
For the best sightseeing on a tour bus, avoid selecting a seat blocked by a panel or a curtain. Often the ideal location is the very back of the bus, where most people don't like to sit, because you usually can move from one side of the bus to the other as needed to get the best view.

ADDING THE APPLIQUÉS

Refer to **Wall Hanging Top Diagram** *for placement.*

1. Arrange appliqués on wall hanging top working from background to foreground in alphabetical order; fuse in place.
2. Machine Blanket Stitch Appliqué pieces to wall hanging top.

FINISHING THE QUILT

1. Follow **Quilting**, page 124, to mark, layer, and quilt as desired. Pat's quilt is outline quilted around the appliqués. The hills are quilted with wavy horizontal lines and the sky has loops and stars. The sheep are quilted with little swirls. There is a continuous petal design quilted in the border.
2. Refer to **Making a Hanging Sleeve**, page 126, to make and attach a hanging sleeve, if desired.
3. Use **binding strips** and follow **Making Straight-Grain Binding**, page 126, to make binding. Follow **Pat's Machine-Sewn Binding**, page 126, to bind wall hanging.

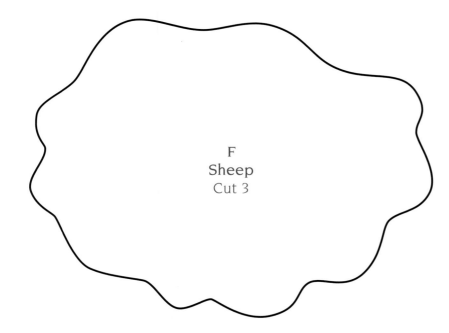

F
Sheep
Cut 3

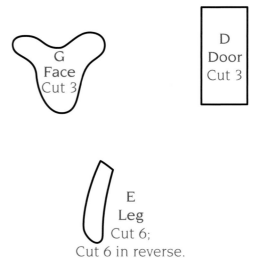

G
Face
Cut 3

D
Door
Cut 3

E
Leg
Cut 6;
Cut 6 in reverse.

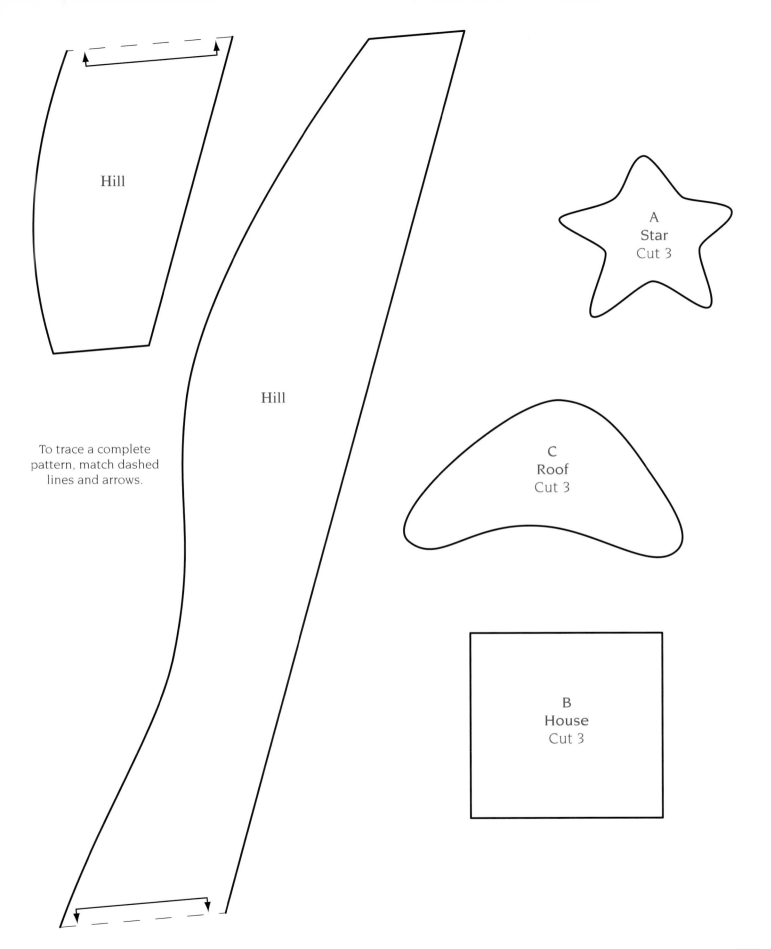

Hill

Hill

To trace a complete pattern, match dashed lines and arrows.

A
Star
Cut 3

C
Roof
Cut 3

B
House
Cut 3

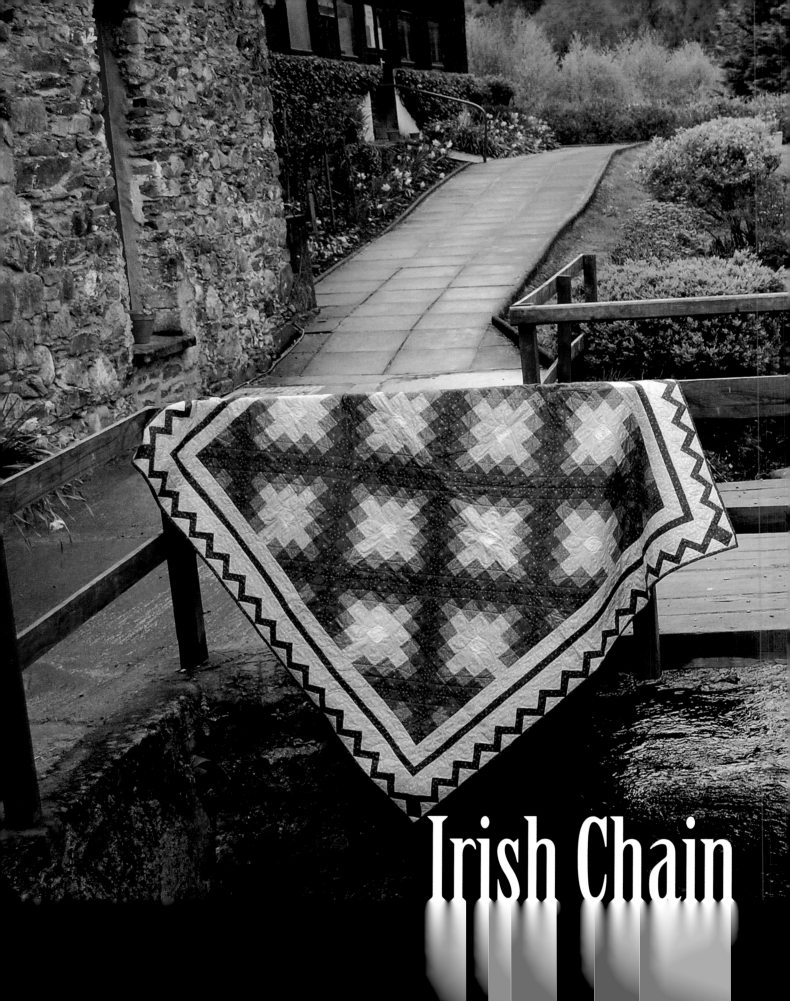

Irish Chain

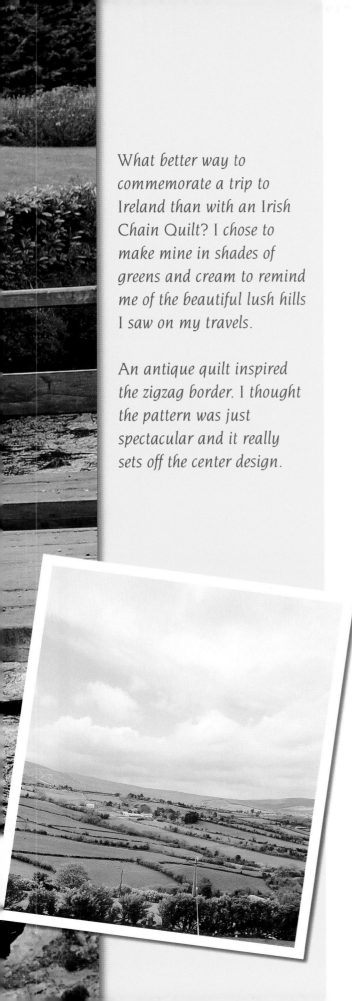

What better way to commemorate a trip to Ireland than with an Irish Chain Quilt? I chose to make mine in shades of greens and cream to remind me of the beautiful lush hills I saw on my travels.

An antique quilt inspired the zigzag border. I thought the pattern was just spectacular and it really sets off the center design.

Finished Quilt Size: 67½" x 67½" (171 cm x 171 cm)
Finished Block Size: 10" x 10" (25 cm x 25 cm)

FABRIC REQUIREMENTS
Yardage is based on 43"/44" (109 cm/112 cm) wide fabric.
   ⅛ yd (11 cm) of cream print fabric #1 (light)
   2⅛ yds (1.9 m) of cream print fabric #2 (medium)
   ⅝ yd (57 cm) of cream print fabric #3 (dark)
   1 yd (91 cm) of green print fabric #1 (light)
   1¼ yds (1.1 m) of green print fabric #2 (medium)
   2 yds (1.8 m) of green print fabric #3 (dark)
   4¼ yds (3.9 m) fabric for backing
You will also need:
   76" x 76" (193 cm x 193 cm) piece of batting

CUTTING THE PIECES
Follow **Rotary Cutting**, *page 120, to cut fabric. Cut all strips from the selvage-to-selvage width of the fabric. All measurements include* ¼" *seam allowances.*
From cream print fabric #1:
- Cut 1 strip 2½" wide.

From cream print fabric #2:
- Cut 4 strips 2½" wide.
- Cut 6 strips 3½" wide. From these strips, cut 66 squares 3½" x 3½". Cut each square **once** diagonally to make 132 **border triangles**.
- Cut 2 squares 2⅜" x 2⅜". Cut each square **once** diagonally to make 4 **border corner triangles**.
- Cut 6 #1 **inner border strips** 2½" wide.
- Cut 6 #3 **inner border strips** 2½" wide.

From cream print fabric #3:
- Cut 8 strips 2½" wide.

From green print fabric #1:
- Cut 12 strips 2½" wide.

From green print fabric #2:
- Cut 16 strips 2½" wide.

From green print fabric #3:
- Cut 9 strips 2½" wide.
- Cut 11 strips 1½" wide. From these strips, cut 132 **short strips** 1½" x 3⅛".
- Cut 4 **corner strips** 1½" x 4⅛".
- Cut 6 #2 **inner border strips** 1½" wide.
- Cut 8 **binding strips** 1½" wide.

ASSEMBLING THE QUILT TOP CENTER

*Follow **Piecing** and **Pressing**, page 121, to make quilt top. Use ¼" seam allowances throughout.*

1. Sew 5 **strips** together to make **Strip Set A**. Cut across Strip Set A at 2½" intervals to make 12 **Unit 1**'s.

Strip Set A (make 1)   **Unit 1** (make 12)

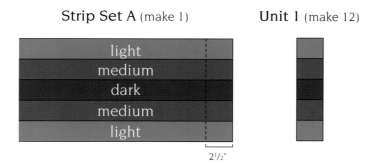

2. Sew 5 **strips** together to make **Strip Set B**. Make 2 Strip Set B's. Cut across Strip Set B at 2½" intervals to make **Unit 2**. Make 24 Unit 2's.

Strip Set B (make 2)   **Unit 2** (make 24)

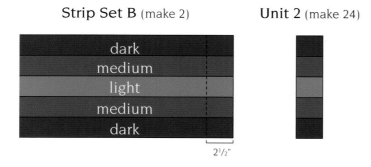

3. Sew 5 **strips** together to make **Strip Set C**. Make 2 Strip Set C's. Cut across Strip Set C at 2½" intervals to make **Unit 3**. Make 24 Unit 3's.

Strip Set C (make 2)   **Unit 3** (make 24)

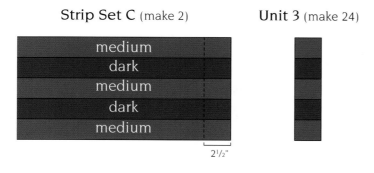

4. Sew 1 **Unit 1**, 2 **Unit 2's**, and 2 **Unit 3's** together to make **Block A**. Make 12 Block A's.

Block A (make 12)

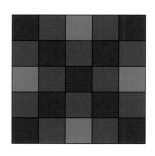

Jim's Travel Tip:
When flying to Ireland, set your watch to Irish time as soon as you get onboard the plane. This will help your mind adjust to the time difference.

5. Sew 5 **strips** together to make **Strip Set D**. Cut across Strip Set D at 2½" intervals to make **Unit 4**. Make 13 Unit 4's.

6. Sew 5 **strips** together to make **Strip Set E**. Make 2 Strip Set E's. Cut across Strip Set E at 2½" intervals to make **Unit 5**. Make 26 Unit 5's.

Strip Set D (make 1)

dark
medium
light
medium
dark

2½"

Unit 4 (make 13)

Strip Set E (make 2)

light
dark
medium
dark
light

2½"

Unit 5 (make 26)

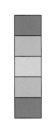

Did anyone get that shot?

May your neighbors respect you,
Trouble neglect you,
The angels protect you,
And heaven accept you.

7. Sew 5 **strips** together to make **Strip Set F**. Make 2 Strip Set F's. Cut across Strip Set F at 2½" intervals to make **Unit 6**. Make 26 Unit 6's.

Strip Set F (make 2)   **Unit 6** (make 26)

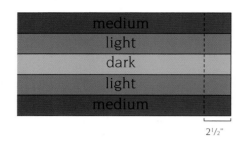 

2½"

8. Sew 1 **Unit 4**, 2 **Unit 5's**, and 2 **Unit 6's** together to make **Block B**. Make 13 Block B's.

Block B (make 13)

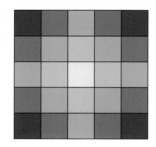

9. Sew 3 **Block A's** and 2 **Block B's** together to make **Row A**. Make 3 Row A's. Sew 2 **Block A's** and 3 **Block B's** together to make **Row B**. Make 2 Row B's.

Row A (make 3)

Row B (make 2)

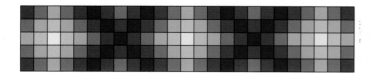

10. Referring to **Quilt Top Diagram**, page 109, sew 3 **Row A's** and 2 **Row B's** together to make quilt top center.

ADDING THE BORDERS
Inner Border
1. Using diagonal seams (**Fig. 1**), sew **#1 inner border strips** together end to end to make 1 continuous inner border.

Fig. 1

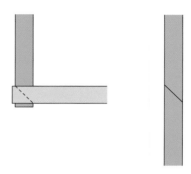

2. To determine length of side #1 inner borders, measure **length** of quilt top center. From #1 inner border strip, cut 2 side #1 inner borders the determined length. Matching centers and corners, sew borders to quilt top center. Press seam allowances toward borders.
3. To determine length of top and bottom #1 inner borders, measure **width** of quilt top center (including added borders). From #1 inner border strip, cut 2 top/bottom #1 inner borders the determined length. Matching centers and corners, sew top and bottom #1 inner borders to quilt top center. Press seam allowances toward borders.
4. Repeat **Steps 1 – 3** to add #2 inner borders.
5. Repeat **Steps 1 – 3** to add #3 inner borders.

Jim's Travel Tip:
When making a trans-Atlantic flight, check in at the airport at least four hours before the plane departs. It's likely you will be one of the first people in line for your flight and it's possible you can change your seat assignment if needed.

Pieced Border

1. Sew 1 green #3 **short strip** to 1 short side of each cream **border triangle** to make **Unit 7** and **Unit 8**. Make 68 Unit 7's and 64 Unit 8's.

Unit 7 (make 68)

Unit 8 (make 64)

2. With Unit 8 on top, sew **Unit 8** to **Unit 7**, beginning at dot and reinforcing stitching (**Fig. 2**).

Fig. 2

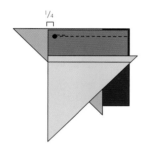

3. Turn pieces just sewn over so that Unit 7 is on top. Fold back point and finger press (**Fig. 3**). Being careful not to catch folded edge of Unit 7 in seam, sew another **Unit 7** to **Unit 8**, ending and reinforcing at dot (**Fig. 4**),

Fig. 3

Fig. 4

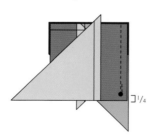

4. Unfold point and complete seam (**Figs. 5** and **6**).

Fig. 5

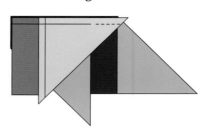

Fig. 6

5. Working left to right, repeat **Steps 2 – 4** to piece border with a total of 17 Unit 7's and 16 Unit 8's (**Fig. 7**).

Fig. 7

6. Sew 1 green **corner strip** to the last Unit 7 sewn to complete 1 pieced border.
7. Repeat **Steps 1 – 6** to make 4 pieced borders.
8. Referring to **Quilt Top Diagram** for orientation, and starting and stopping ¹/₄" from each corner, sew borders to center section of quilt top, easing if necessary.
9. To miter corners, match right sides and raw edges and fold 1 corner of quilt top diagonally. Pin in place, then sew diagonally from corner of border to corner of quilt (**Fig. 8**), reinforcing stitching.

Fig. 8

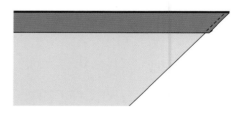

10. Sew 1 cream **border corner triangle** to each corner of quilt top.

FINISHING THE QUILT

1. Following **Quilting**, page 124, to mark, layer, and quilt as desired. Pat's quilt is machine quilted with a flower in the cream areas of each block, diagonal lines along each "chain", and feathers in each border. There is quilting in the ditch along each border and the outside edges of the zigzag borders.

2. Refer to **Making A Hanging Sleeve**, page 126, to make and attach a hanging sleeve, if desired.

3. Use **binding strips** and follow **Making Straight-Grain Binding**, page 126, to make binding. Follow **Pat's Machine-Sewn Binding**, page 126, to bind quilt.

Quilt Top Diagram

Jim's Travel Tip:
One of the best and least expensive gifts to bring back to family and friends are jams and jellies purchased at a local grocery store (not a specialty shop).

Streets of Ireland

Every little town we visited was dotted with old-world style street signs. Sometimes the signs pointed to other towns and sometimes to places within the town, such as famous landmarks, buildings, or restaurants.

I created this quilt, complete with the names of some of the places we visited, to capture the memory of these wonderful signs. The pot of pretty blooms serves as a reminder of the beautiful flowers we saw everywhere and that we were lucky enough to experience an early Irish spring.

Finished Size: 34½" x 41½"
(88 cm x 105 cm)

FABRIC REQUIREMENTS

Yardage is based on 43"/44" (109 cm/112 cm) wide fabric.

- 24½" x 18½" (62 cm x 47 cm) piece of light blue print fabric for background
- 24½" x 13" (62 cm x 33 cm) piece of green print fabric for background
- ½ yd (46 cm) of rust print #1 fabric for inner border and binding
- ¾ yd (69 cm) of brown floral print fabric for outer border
- 15" x 14" (38 cm x 36 cm) piece of tan print fabric for large house appliqué
- 11" x 11" (28 cm x 28 cm) square of rust print #2 fabric for small house appliqué
- 12" x 12" (30 cm x 30 cm) square of blue print fabric for sign appliqués
- 2½" x 31" (6 cm x 79 cm) piece of black print #1 fabric for signpost and chimney appliqués
- 3¾" x 12" (10 cm x 30 cm) piece of black print #2 fabric for rim of signpost base appliqué
- 11" x 3½" (28 cm x 9 cm) piece of grey print fabric for signpost base
- 4½" x 16" (11 cm x 41 cm) piece **each** of 2 brown print fabrics for roof appliqués
- Scraps of assorted print fabrics for remaining appliqués
- 1⅜ yds (1.3 m) of fabric for backing

You will also need:

- 39" x 46" (99 cm x 117 cm) rectangle of batting
- Paper-backed fusible web
- ½" (13 mm) diameter black button for doorknob
- 9⁄16" (14 mm) diameter black button for doorknob
- Cream #8 pearl cotton
- Chalk-based marking pencil
- Stabilizer or spray starch

CUTTING THE PIECES

*Follow **Rotary Cutting**, page 120, to cut fabric. Cut all strips from the selvage-to-selvage width of the fabric. All measurements include 1/4" seam allowances.*

From rust print #1 fabric:
- Cut 2 **inner top/bottom borders** 1 1/4" x 24 1/2".
- Cut 2 **inner side borders** 1 1/4" x 32 1/2".
- Cut 5 **binding strips** 1 1/2" wide.

From brown floral print fabric:
- Cut 2 **outer top/bottom borders** 4 1/2" x 26".
- Cut 2 **outer side borders** 4 1/2" x 41", pieced if needed.

CUTTING THE APPLIQUÉS

*Patterns on pages 115-119 are reversed and do not include seam allowances. Follow **Preparing Fusible Appliqués**, page 122, to cut appliqués.*

From tan print fabric:
- Cut 1 **large house (C)** 14 1/4" x 13 1/4".

From rust print #2 fabric:
- Cut 1 **small house (A)** 10" x 9 7/8".

From blue print fabric:
- Cut 3 **signs (N)**.

From black print #1 fabric:
- Cut 1 **signpost (M)** 1 1/4" x 27 1/4".
- Cut 1 **chimney (D)** 1 1/4" x 2 7/8".

From black print #2 fabric:
- Cut 1 **rim of signpost base (K)**.

From grey print fabric:
- Cut 1 **signpost base (J)** 10 3/4" x 3".

From brown print fabrics:
- Cut 1 **large roof (E)**.
- Cut 1 **small roof (B)**.

From assorted scrap print fabrics:
- Cut 5 **large house windows (H)** 2" x 3 5/8".
- Cut 1 **large house door (I)**.
- Cut 5 **small house windows (F)** 1 3/4" x 3 1/4".
- Cut 1 **small house door (G)**.
- Cut 1 **inside signpost base (L)**.
- Cut 1 **flower barrel (O)**.
- Cut 6 **leaves (P)**.
- Cut 6 **flowers (Q)**.
- Cut 6 **flower centers (R)**.

ASSEMBLING THE QUILT TOP CENTER

*Refer to **Piecing** and **Pressing**, page 121, to assemble quilt top. Use 1/4" seam allowances throughout.*

1. Sew the light blue and green **rectangles** together to make background (**Fig. 1**).

Fig. 1

ADDING THE APPLIQUÉS

*Refer to the **Quilt Top Diagram**, page 114, for appliqué placement. Refer to **Machine Blanket Stitch Appliqué**, page 122, for technique. It is not necessary to appliqué edges of appliqués that extend to the edge of the background; these will be sewn into the seam when the inner border is added.*

1. Arrange all appliqué pieces except flower barrel, flowers, flower centers, leaves, and signpost parts on background working in alphabetical order; fuse in place.
2. Machine Blanket Stitch Appliqué pieces to background to make quilt top center.

ADDING THE BORDERS

1. Matching centers and corners, sew inner top/ bottom borders to quilt top center. Press seam allowances toward borders.
2. Matching centers and corners, sew inner side borders to quilt top center. Press seam allowances toward borders.
3. Repeat **Steps 1-2** to add outer borders.

FINISHING THE QUILT

1. Arrange flower barrel, flowers, flower centers, leaves, and signpost parts; fuse in place.
2. Machine Blanket Stitch Appliqué pieces to quilt top center.
3. Use marking pencil to write town names on signs. Use a Stem Stitch, page 128, to embroidery the town names on the signs.
4. Following **Quilting**, page 124, to mark, layer, and quilt the quilt top. Pat's quilt is quilted with clouds in the sky, scallops on the roofs, vertical lines on the houses, horizontal lines on the grass, bubbles on the signpost base and big leaves and swirls in the border. The windowpanes and smoke in the chimney are all machine quilted. You could embroider them for a different look, if desired.
5. Refer to **Making A Hanging Sleeve**, page 126, to make and attach a hanging sleeve if desired.
6. Use binding strips and follow **Making Straight-Grain Binding**, page 126, to make binding. Follow **Pat's Machine-Sewn Binding**, page 126, to bind quilt.
7. Sew buttons to doors for doorknobs.

Quilt Top Diagram

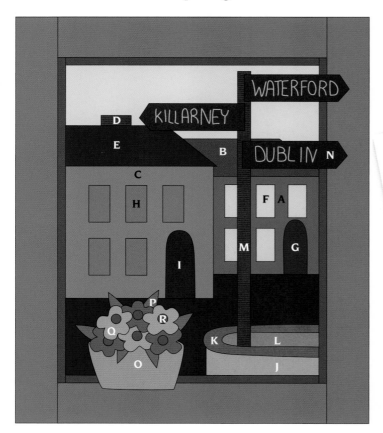

Jim's Travel Tip:
Shopping is great in Ireland. The Blarney Woolen Mills is a wonderful place to purchase all kinds of items, from Waterford Crystal to woolen sweaters and everything else "Irish." A good rule of thumb when shopping abroad is, if you see it and like it and you think it's a good price, buy it. You may not see it again.

114

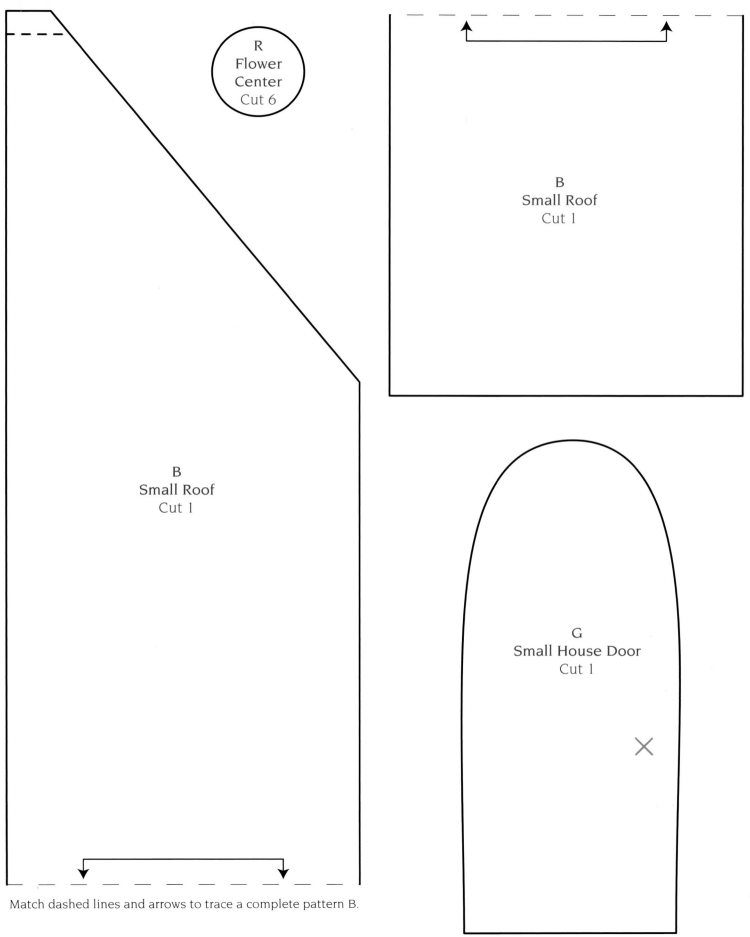

R
Flower
Center
Cut 6

B
Small Roof
Cut 1

B
Small Roof
Cut 1

G
Small House Door
Cut 1

Match dashed lines and arrows to trace a complete pattern B.

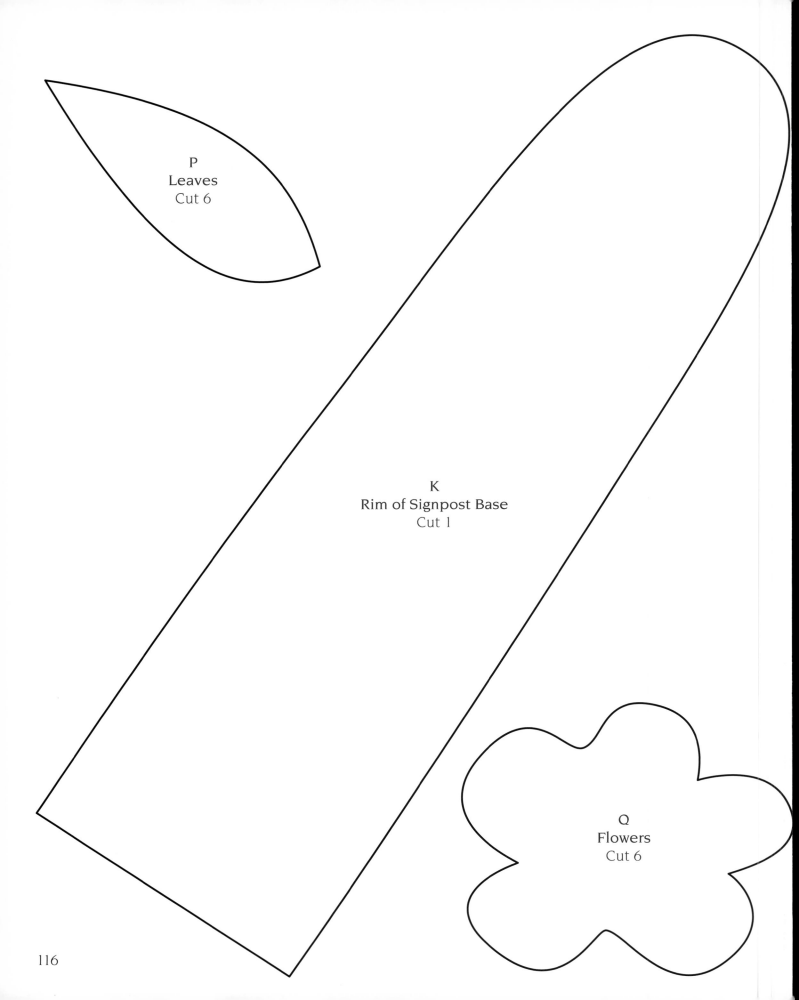

P
Leaves
Cut 6

K
Rim of Signpost Base
Cut 1

Q
Flowers
Cut 6

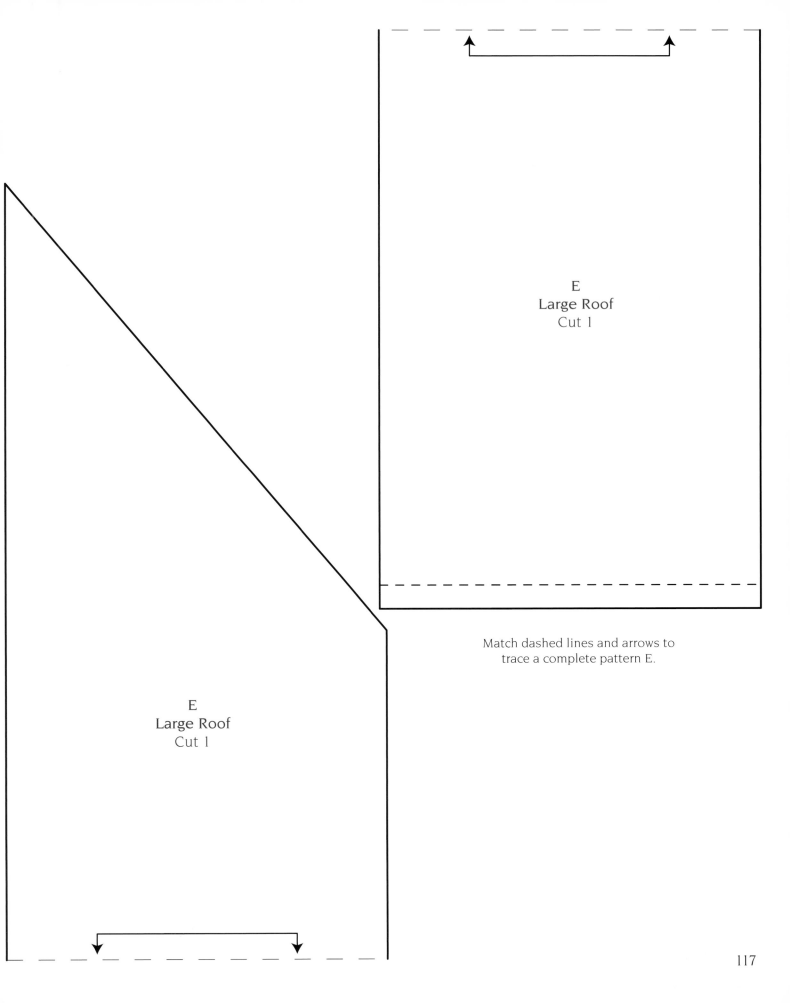

E
Large Roof
Cut 1

Match dashed lines and arrows to
trace a complete pattern E.

E
Large Roof
Cut 1

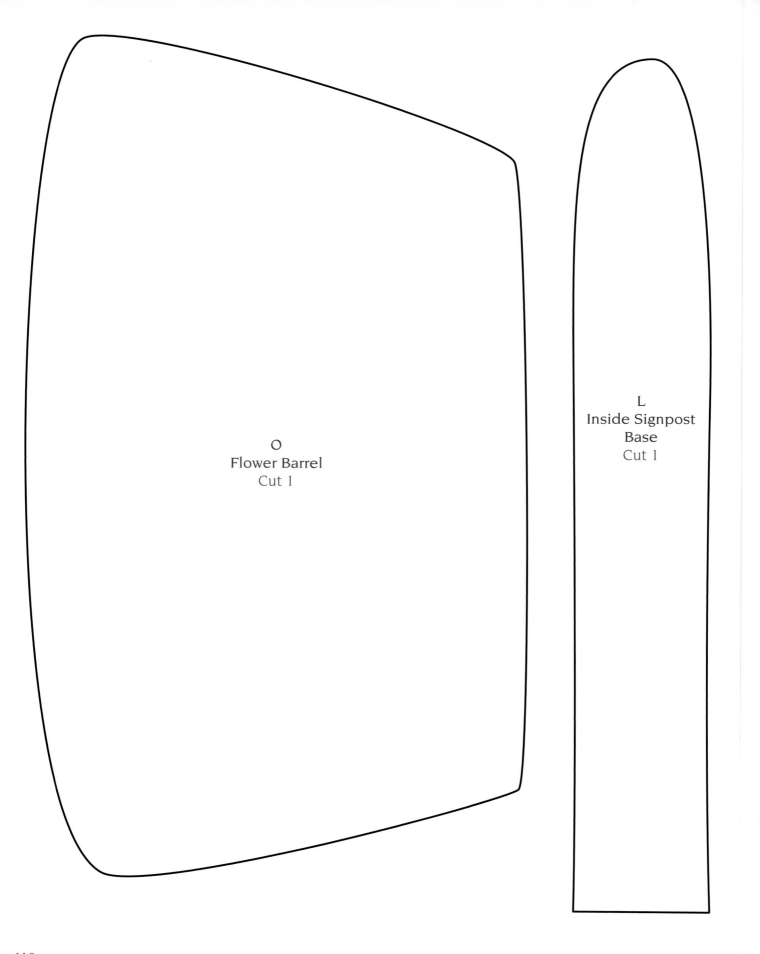

O
Flower Barrel
Cut 1

L
Inside Signpost
Base
Cut 1

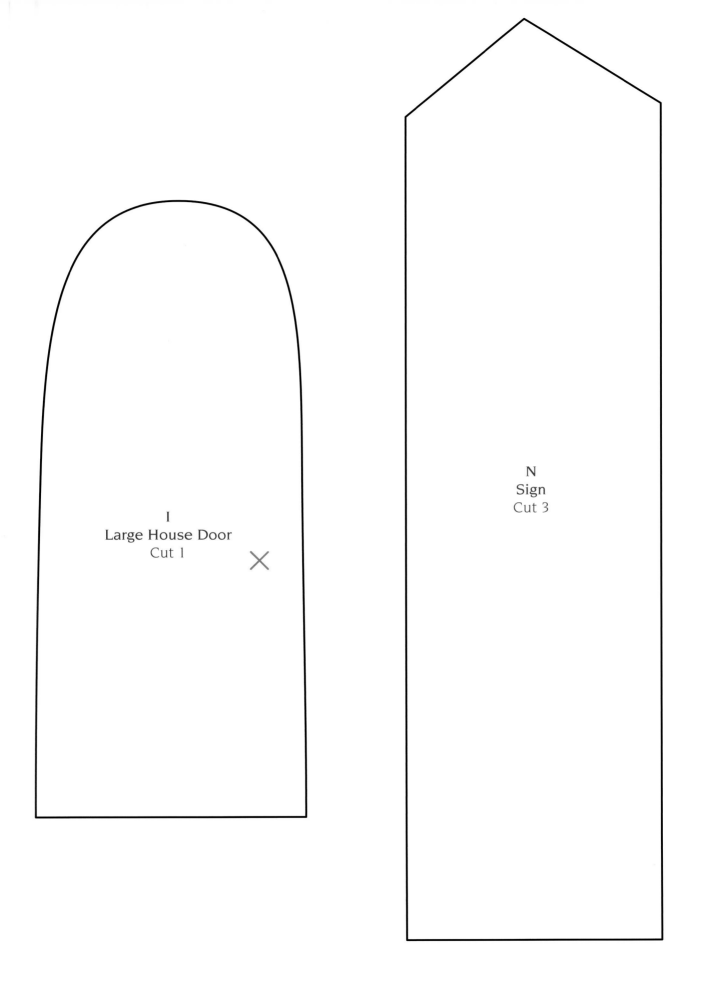

I
Large House Door
Cut 1

N
Sign
Cut 3

General Instructions

To make your quilting easier and more enjoyable, we encourage you to carefully read all of the general instructions, study the color photographs, and familiarize yourself with the individual project instructions before beginning a project.

FABRICS

SELECTING FABRICS

Choose high-quality, medium-weight 100% cotton fabrics. All-cotton fabrics hold a crease better, fray less, and are easier to quilt than cotton/polyester blends.

Yardage requirements listed for each project are based on 43"/44" wide fabric with a "usable" width of 40" after shrinkage and trimming selvages. Actual usable width will probably vary slightly from fabric to fabric. Our recommended yardage lengths should be adequate for occasional re-squaring of fabric when many cuts are required.

PREPARING FABRICS

We recommend that all fabrics be washed, dried, and pressed before cutting. If fabrics are not pre-washed, washing the finished quilt will cause shrinkage and give it a more "antiqued" look and feel. Bright and dark colors, which may run, should always be washed before cutting. After washing and drying fabric, fold lengthwise with wrong sides together and matching selvages.

ROTARY CUTTING

Rotary cutting has brought speed and accuracy to quiltmaking by allowing quilters to easily cut strips of fabric and then cut those strips into smaller pieces.

- Place fabric on work surface with fold closest to you.

- Cut all strips from the selvage-to-selvage width of the fabric unless otherwise indicated in project instructions.

- Square left edge of fabric using rotary cutter and rulers (**Figs. 1 - 2**).

- To cut each strip required for a project, place ruler over cut edge of fabric, aligning desired marking on ruler with cut edge; make cut (**Fig. 3**).

- When cutting several strips from a single piece of fabric, it is important to make sure that cuts remain at a perfect right angle to the fold; square fabric as needed.

Fig. 1

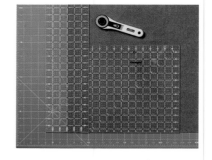

Fig. 2

Fig. 3

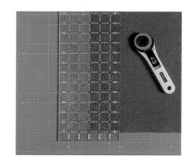

TEMPLATE CUTTING

Patterns for appliqué templates do not include seam allowances. When cutting instructions say to cut in reverse, place the template upside down on the fabric to cut piece in reverse.

1. To make a template from a pattern, use a permanent fine-point pen and a ruler to carefully trace pattern onto template plastic, making sure to transfer any markings. Cut out template along inner edge of drawn line. Check template against original pattern for accuracy.

2. Place template on right side of appliqué fabric. Use a pencil to lightly draw around template, leaving at least 1/2" between shapes; repeat for number of appliqués specified in project instructions. Cut out shapes 1/4" outside drawn line.

PIECING

Precise cutting, followed by accurate piecing, will ensure that all pieces of quilt top fit together well.

- Set sewing machine stitch length for approximately 11 stitches per inch.

- Use neutral-colored general-purpose sewing thread (not quilting thread) in needle and in bobbin.

- An accurate 1/4" seam allowance is essential. Presser feet that are 1/4" wide are available for most sewing machines.

- When piecing, always place pieces right sides together and match raw edges; pin if necessary.

- Chain piecing saves time and will usually result in more accurate piecing.

- Trim away points of seam allowances that extend beyond edges of sewn pieces.

SEWING STRIP SETS

When there are several strips to assemble into a strip set, first sew strips together into pairs, then sew pairs together to form strip set. To help avoid distortion, sew seams in opposite directions (**Fig. 4**).

Fig. 4

SEWING ACROSS SEAM INTERSECTIONS

When sewing across intersection of two seams, place pieces right sides together and match seams exactly, making sure seam allowances are pressed in opposite directions (**Fig. 5**).

Fig. 5

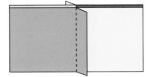

SEWING SHARP POINTS

To ensure sharp points when joining triangular or diagonal pieces, stitch across the center of the "X" (shown in pink) formed on wrong side by previous seams (**Fig. 6**).

Fig. 6

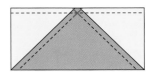

PRESSING

- Use steam iron set on "Cotton" for all pressing.

- Press after sewing each seam.

- Seam allowances are almost always pressed to one side, usually toward darker fabric. However, to reduce bulk it may occasionally be necessary to press seam allowances toward the lighter fabric or even to press them open.

- To prevent dark fabric seam allowance from showing through light fabric, trim darker seam allowance slightly narrower than lighter seam allowance.

- To press long seams, such as those in long strip sets, without curving or other distortion, lay strips across width of the ironing board.

MACHINE APPLIQUÉ
PREPARING FUSIBLE APPLIQUÉS

Patterns for fused appliqués are printed in reverse to enable you to use our speedy method of preparing appliqués by following **Steps** 1 – 4 *(below). If the instructions call for a pattern to be cut in reverse, it is because the shape will be used facing both directions. Use a black fine-point marker to trace the pattern onto plain white paper, flip paper over and then follow* **Steps** 1 – 4 *to trace pattern onto web from the "wrong" side of the paper.*

1. Place paper-backed fusible web, web side down, over appliqué pattern. Use a pencil to trace pattern onto paper side of web as many times as indicated in project instructions for a single fabric. Repeat for additional patterns and fabrics. (**Note:** Some pieces may be given as measurements, such as a 2" x 4" rectangle, instead of drawn patterns. Draw shape onto paper side of web using ruler.)

2. To reduce stiffness when appliquéing, cut away the center of the fusible web ¼" inside the traced line. Do not cut on the line (**Fig. 7**). It may not be necessary to cut away the center of small or narrow pieces.

3. Follow manufacturer's instructions to fuse traced patterns to wrong side of fabrics. Do not remove paper backing.

4. Cut out appliqué pieces along traced lines (**Fig. 8**). Remove paper backing from all pieces (**Fig. 9**).

Fig. 7

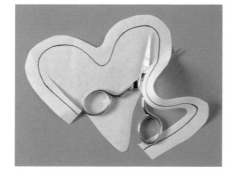

Fig. 8

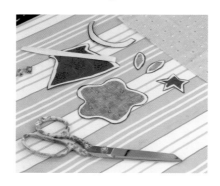

Fig. 9

MACHINE BLANKET STITCH APPLIQUÉ

Some sewing machines feature a Blanket Stitch similar to the one used in this book. Refer to your owner's manual for machine set-up. If your machine does not have this stitch, try any of the decorative stitches your machine has until you are satisfied with the look.

1. Thread sewing machine and bobbin with 100% cotton thread in desired weight.

2. Attach an open-toe presser foot. Select far right needle position and needle down (if your machine has these features).

3. If desired, pin a commercial stabilizer to wrong side of background fabric or spray wrong side of background fabric with starch to stabilize.

4. Bring bobbin thread to the top of the fabric by lowering then raising the needle, bringing up the bobbin thread loop. Pull the loop all the way to the surface.

5. Begin by stitching 5 or 6 stitches in place (drop feed dogs or set stitch length at 0), or use your machine's lock stitch feature, if equipped, to anchor thread. Return setting to selected Blanket Stitch.

6. Most of the Blanket Stitch should be done on the appliqué with the right edges of the stitch falling at the very outside edge of the appliqué. Stitch over all exposed raw edges of appliqué pieces.

7. (**Note**: Dots on **Figs. 10 – 14** indicate where to leave needle in fabric when pivoting.) Always stopping with needle down in background fabric, refer to **Fig. 10** to stitch outside points like tips of leaves. Stop one stitch short of point. Raise presser foot. Pivot project slightly, lower presser foot, and make one angled **Stitch** 1. Take next stitch, stop at point, and pivot so **Stitch 2** will be perpendicular to point. Pivot slightly to make **Stitch 3**. Continue stitching.

Fig. 10

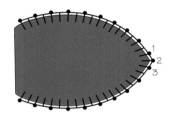

8. For outside corners (**Fig. 11**), stitch to corner, stopping with needle in background fabric. Raise presser foot. Pivot project, lower presser foot, and take an angled stitch. Raise presser foot. Pivot project, lower presser foot and stitch adjacent side.

Fig. 11

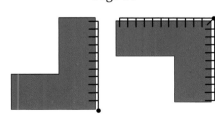

9. For inside corners (**Fig. 12**), stitch to the corner, taking the last bite at corner and stopping with the needle down in background fabric. Raise presser foot. Pivot project, lower presser foot, and take an angled stitch. Raise presser foot. Pivot project, lower presser foot and stitch adjacent side.

Fig. 12

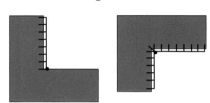

10. When stitching outside curves (**Fig. 13**), stop with needle down in background fabric. Raise presser foot and pivot project as needed. Lower presser foot and continue stitching, pivoting as often as necessary to follow curve. Small circles may require pivoting between each stitch.

Fig. 13

11. When stitching inside curves (**Fig. 14**), stop with needle down in background fabric. Raise presser foot and pivot project as needed. Lower presser foot and continue stitching, pivoting as often as necessary to follow curve.

Fig. 14

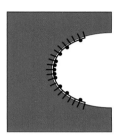

12. When stopping stitching, use a lock stitch to sew 5 or 6 stitches in place or use a needle to pull threads to wrong side of background fabric (**Fig. 15**); knot, then trim ends.

Fig. 15

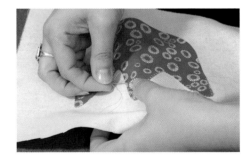

13. Carefully tear away stabilizer, if used.

QUILTING

Quilting holds the three layers (top, batting, and backing) of the quilt together and can be done by hand or machine. Because marking, layering, and quilting are interrelated and may be done in different orders depending on circumstances, please read entire Quilting section, pages 124 – 126, before beginning project.

TYPES OF QUILTING DESIGNS

In the Ditch Quilting
Quilting along seamlines or along edges of appliquéd pieces is called "in the ditch" quilting. This type of quilting should be done on side opposite seam allowance and does not have to be marked.

Outline Quilting
Quilting a consistent distance, usually ¹/₄", from seam or appliqué is called "outline" quilting. Outline quilting may be marked, or ¹/₄" masking tape may be placed along seamlines for quilting guide. (Do not leave tape on quilt longer than necessary, since it may leave an adhesive residue.)

Motif Quilting
Quilting a design, such as a feathered wreath, is called "motif" quilting. This type of quilting should be marked before basting quilt layers together.

Echo Quilting
Quilting that follows the outline of an appliquéd or pieced design with two or more parallel lines is called "echo" quilting. This type of quilting does not need to be marked.

Channel Quilting
Quilting with straight, parallel lines is called "channel" quilting. This type of quilting may be marked or stitched using a guide.

Crosshatch Quilting
Quilting straight lines in a grid pattern is called "crosshatch" quilting. Lines may be stitched parallel to edges of quilt or stitched diagonally. This type of quilting may be marked or stitched using a guide.

Meandering Quilting
Quilting in random curved lines and swirls is called "meandering" quilting. Quilting lines should not cross or touch each other. This type of quilting does not need to be marked.

Stipple Quilting
Meandering quilting that is very closely spaced is called "stipple" quilting. Stippling will flatten the area quilted and is often stitched in background areas to raise appliquéd or pieced designs. This type of quilting does not need to be marked.

MARKING QUILTING LINES
Quilting lines may be marked using fabric marking pencils, chalk markers, water- or air-soluble pens, or lead pencils.

Simple quilting designs may be marked with chalk or chalk pencil after basting. A small area may be marked, then quilted, before moving to next area to be marked. Intricate designs should be marked before basting using a more durable marker.

Caution: Pressing may permanently set some marks. Test different markers on scrap fabric to find one that marks clearly and can be thoroughly removed.

A wide variety of pre-cut quilting stencils, as well as entire books of quilting patterns, are available. Using a stencil makes it easier to mark intricate or repetitive designs.

To make a stencil from a pattern, center template plastic over pattern and use a permanent marker to trace pattern onto plastic. Use a craft knife with single or double blade to cut channels along traced lines (**Fig. 16**).

Fig. 16

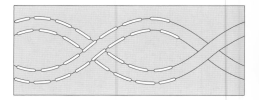

PREPARING THE BACKING
To allow for slight shifting of quilt top during quilting, backing should be approximately 4" larger on all sides. Yardage requirements listed for quilt backings are calculated for 43"/44"w fabric. Using 90"w or 108"w fabric for the backing of a bed-sized quilt may eliminate piecing. To piece a backing using 43"/44"w fabric, use the following instructions.

1. Measure length and width of quilt top; add 8" to each measurement.

2. Cut backing fabric into 2 or 3 lengths (depending on quilt size) the determined *length* measurement. Trim selvages. Place lengths with right sides facing and sew long edges together, forming tube (**Fig. 17**). Match seams and press along one fold (**Fig. 18**). Cut along pressed fold to form single piece (**Fig. 19**).

Fig. 17   Fig. 18   Fig. 19

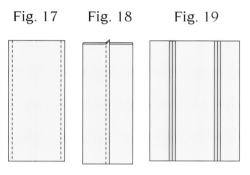

3. Trim backing to size determined in Step 1; press seam allowances open.

CHOOSING THE BATTING

The appropriate batting will make quilting easier. For fine hand quilting, choose low-loft batting. All cotton or cotton/polyester blend battings work well for machine quilting because the cotton helps "grip" quilt layers. If quilt is to be tied, a high-loft batting, sometimes called extra-loft or fat batting, may be used to make quilt "fluffy."

Types of batting include cotton, polyester, cotton/polyester blend, wool, cotton/wool blend, and silk.

When selecting batting, refer to package labels for characteristics and care instructions. Cut batting same size as prepared backing.

ASSEMBLING THE QUILT

1. Examine wrong side of quilt top closely; trim any seam allowances and clip any threads that may show through front of the quilt. Press quilt top, being careful not to "set" any marked quilting lines.
2. Place backing wrong side up on flat surface. Use masking tape to tape edges of backing to surface. Place batting on top of backing fabric. Smooth batting gently, being careful not to stretch or tear. Center quilt top right side up on batting.
3. Use 1" rustproof safety pins to "pin-baste" all layers together, spacing pins approximately 4" apart. Begin at center and work toward outer edges to secure all layers. If possible, place pins away from areas that will be quilted, although pins may be removed as needed when quilting.

MACHINE QUILTING METHODS

Using the same color general-purpose thread in the needle and bobbin avoids "dots" of bobbin thread being pulled to the surface. Use a general-purpose thread in the bobbin and a decorative thread for stitching, such as metallic, variegated or contrasting-colored general-purpose thread, when you desire the quilting to be more pronounced.

Straight-Line Quilting
The term "straight-line" is somewhat deceptive, since curves (especially gentle ones) as well as straight lines can be stitched with this technique.

1. Set stitch length for six to ten stitches per inch and attach walking foot to sewing machine.
2. Determine which section of quilt will have longest continuous quilting line, oftentimes area from center top to center bottom. Roll up and secure each edge of quilt to help reduce the bulk, keeping fabrics smooth. Smaller projects may not need to be rolled.
3. Begin stitching on longest quilting line, using very short stitches for the first ¼" to "lock" quilting. Stitch across project, using one hand on each side of walking foot to slightly spread fabric and to guide fabric through machine. Lock stitches at end of quilting line.
4. Continue machine quilting, stitching longer quilting lines first to stabilize quilt before moving on to other areas.

Free-Motion Quilting
Free-motion quilting may be free form or may follow a marked pattern.

1. Attach darning foot to sewing machine and lower or cover feed dogs.

2. Position quilt under darning foot; lower foot. Holding top thread, take a stitch and pull bobbin thread to top of quilt. To "lock" beginning of quilting line, hold top and bobbin threads while making three to five stitches in place.

3. Use one hand on each side of darning foot to slightly spread fabric and to move fabric through the machine. Even stitch length is achieved by using smooth, flowing hand motion and steady machine speed. Slow machine speed and fast hand movement will create long stitches. Fast machine speed and slow hand movement will create short stitches. Move quilt sideways, back and forth, in a circular motion, or in a random motion to create desired designs; do not rotate quilt. Lock stitches at end of each quilting line.

MAKING A HANGING SLEEVE

Attaching a hanging sleeve to back of wall hanging or quilt before the binding is added allows project to be displayed on wall.

1. Measure width of quilt top edge and subtract 1". Cut piece of fabric 7"w by determined measurement.

2. Press short edges of fabric piece $\frac{1}{4}$" to wrong side; press edges $\frac{1}{4}$" to wrong side again and machine stitch in place.

3. Matching wrong sides, fold piece in half lengthwise to form tube.

4. Follow project instructions to sew binding to quilt top and to trim backing and batting. Before Blindstitching binding to backing, match raw edges and stitch hanging sleeve to center top edge on back of quilt.

5. Finish binding quilt, treating hanging sleeve as part of backing.

6. Blindstitch bottom of hanging sleeve to backing, taking care not to stitch through to front of quilt.

7. Insert dowel or slat into hanging sleeve.

BINDING
MAKING STRAIGHT-GRAIN BINDING

1. With right sides together and using diagonal seams (**Fig. 20**), sew the short ends of binding strips together, if needed, to achieve the necessary length.

Fig. 20

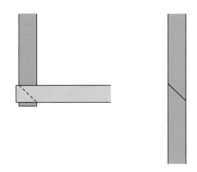

2. Press seam allowances open. Press one long edge of binding 1/4" to the wrong side.

PAT'S MACHINE-SEWN BINDING

For a quick and easy finish when attaching straight-grain binding with overlapped corners, Pat sews her binding to the back of the quilt and Machine Blanket Stitches it in place on the front, eliminating all hand stitching.

1. Using a narrow zigzag, stitch around quilt close to the raw edges (**Fig. 21**). Trim backing and batting even with edges of quilt top.

Fig. 21

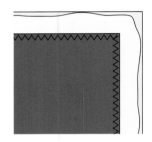

2. Matching raw edges and using a $\frac{1}{4}$" seam allowance, sew a length of binding to top and bottom edges on wrong side of quilt.

3. Fold binding over to quilt front and pin pressed edge in place, covering stitching line. Blanket Stitch binding close to pressed edge (**Fig. 22**). Trim ends of top and bottom binding even with edges of quilt top.

Fig. 22

4. Leaving approximately 1½" of binding at each end, stitch a length of binding to wrong side of each side of quilt (**Fig. 23**).

Fig. 23

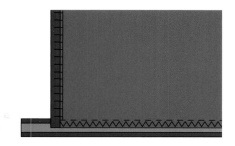

5. Trim each end of binding ½" longer than bound edge. Fold under each raw end of binding (**Fig. 24**); pin in place. Fold binding over to quilt front and Blanket Stitch in place, as in Step 3.

Fig. 24

SIGNING AND DATING YOUR QUILT

A completed quilt is a work of art and should be signed and dated. There are many different ways to do this and numerous books on the subject. The label should reflect the style of the quilt, the occasion or person for which it was made, and the quilter's own particular talents. Following are suggestions for recording the history of quilt or adding a sentiment for future generations.

- For Pat's Celtic Knot label, trace pattern, below, onto fabric using a light box or brightly lit window. Paint it, embroider it, or color it with colored pencils or fabric markers.

- Embroider quilter's name, date, and any additional information on quilt top or backing. Matching floss, such as cream floss on white border, will leave a subtle record. Bright or contrasting floss will make the information stand out.

- Make label from muslin and use permanent marker to write information. Use different colored permanent markers to make label more decorative. Stitch label to back of quilt.

- Use photo-transfer paper to add image to white or cream fabric label. Stitch label to back of quilt.

- Piece an extra block from quilt top pattern to use as label. Add information with permanent fabric pen. Appliqué block to back of quilt.

- Write message on appliquéd design from quilt top. Attach appliqué to back of the quilt.

Celtic Knot Label

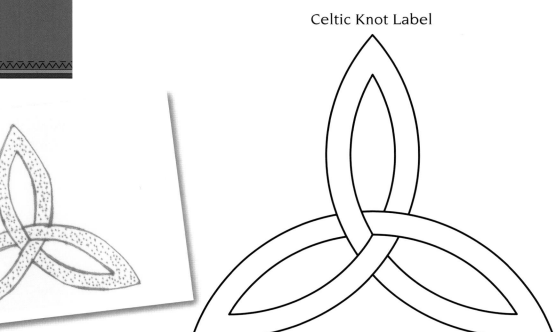

HAND STITCHES
BLANKET STITCH
Come up at 1, go down at 2, and come up at 3, keeping thread below point of needle (**Fig. 25**).

Fig. 25

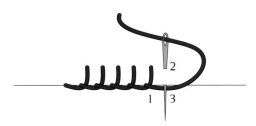

RUNNING STITCH
The running stitch consists of a series of straight stitches with the stitch length equal to the space between stitches. Come up at 1, go down at 2 (**Fig. 27**).

Fig. 27

BLIND STITCH
Come up at 1, go down at 2, and come up at 3 (**Fig. 26**). Length of stitches may be varied as desired.

Fig. 26

STEM STITCH
Come up at 1. Keeping thread below the stitching line, go down at 2 and come up at 3. Go down at 4 and come up at 5 (**Fig. 28**).

Fig. 28

Metric Conversion Chart

Inches x 2.54 = centimeters (cm)	Yards x .9144 = meters (m)
Inches x 25.4 = millimeters (mm)	Yards x 91.44 = centimeters (cm)
Inches x .0254 = meters (m)	Centimeters x .3937 = inches (")
	Meters x 1.0936 = yards (yd)

Standard Equivalents

1/8"	3.2 mm	0.32 cm	1/8 yard	11.43 cm	0.11 m
1/4"	6.35 mm	0.635 cm	1/4 yard	22.86 cm	0.23 m
3/8"	9.5 mm	0.95 cm	3/8 yard	34.29 cm	0.34 m
1/2"	12.7 mm	1.27 cm	1/2 yard	45.72 cm	0.46 m
5/8"	15.9 mm	1.59 cm	5/8 yard	57.15 cm	0.57 m
3/4"	19.1 mm	1.91 cm	3/4 yard	68.58 cm	0.69 m
7/8"	22.2 mm	2.22 cm	7/8 yard	80 cm	0.8 m
1"	25.4 mm	2.54 cm	1 yard	91.44 cm	0.91 m

Many thanks to the companies who provided the supplies needed to make the projects in this book. I used fabrics from P & B Textiles, Mettler® thread, HeatnBondLite® fusible web, Mountain Mist® batting and sewed on a Janome sewing machine.